Corrective Reading

SRA Comprehension Skills

Comprehension B1 Fast Cycle

Siegfried Engelmann

Steve Osborn

Susan Hanner

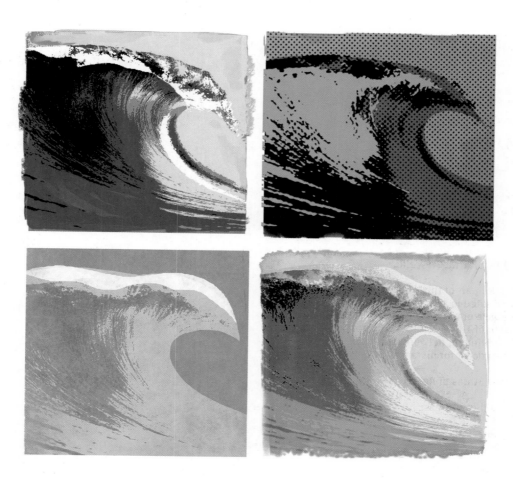

 McGraw Hill SRA

Columbus, OH

SRAonline.com

Send all inquiries to this address:
SRA/McGraw-Hill
4400 Easton Commons
Columbus, OH 43219

ISBN: 978-0-07-611173-2
MHID: 0-07-611173-3

3 4 5 6 7 8 9 QPD 13 12 11 10 09 08

The McGraw·Hill Companies

A BODY SYSTEMS

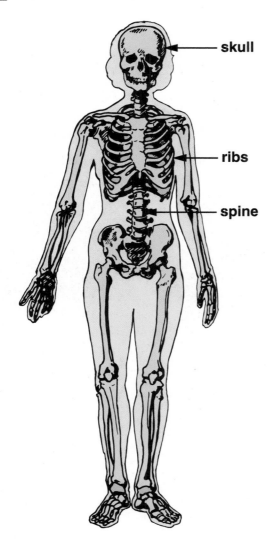

- skull
- ribs
- spine

B FOLLOWING DIRECTIONS

Follow the directions.

1. Draw a horizontal line in the box.

2. Draw a slanted line under the right end of the horizontal line.

3. Draw a slanted line above the left end of the horizontal line.

C INFERENCE

Read the sentence and answer the questions.

The ribs are in front of the spine.

1. Where are the ribs?

_____

2. Is the spine in back of the ribs?

_____

3. What are the ribs in front of?

_____

4. What is in back of the ribs?

_____

D **CLASSIFICATION**

Circle each vehicle. Cross out each container.

A FOLLOWING DIRECTIONS

Follow the directions.

1. Draw a vertical line in the box.

2. Draw a horizontal line above the vertical line.

3. Draw a slanted line under the vertical line.

B EVIDENCE

Write the letter of the fact that explains why each thing happened.

> **A.** The man lived on a ship.
> **B.** The man was a robber.

1. His home was not on a street. _____

2. He was wanted by the cops. _____

3. He picked a lock. _____

4. He had to swim to get to his home. _____

C PARTS OF SPEECH

Underline each part that names. Then circle the noun in that part.

1. The man stood on a rock.

2. Three men stood on a rock.

3. Bill stood near a lake.

4. My little sister was next to me.

5. One boy is very tired.

6. A train is a vehicle.

7. Trains have wheels.

8. Five mean goats chased the farmer.

D INFERENCE

Read the sentence and answer the questions.

A big container can hold lots of things.

1. What can hold lots of things?

   _____

2. What can a big container hold?

   _____

3. How many things can a big container hold?

   _____

   _____

4. What kind of container can hold lots of things?

   _____

E CLASSIFICATION

Underline each container. Cross out each vehicle.

D BODY SYSTEMS

Write **spine, ribs,** or **skull** in each blank.

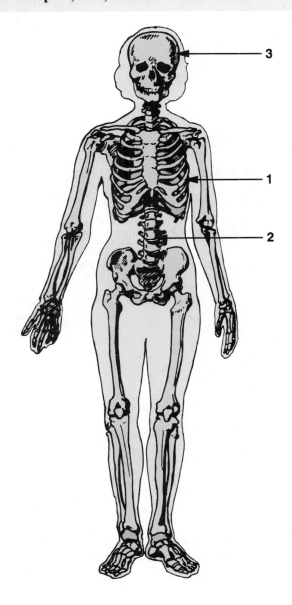

1. _____

2. _____

3. _____

E INFERENCE

Read the sentence and answer the questions.

> Your ribs protect your chest when you fall down.

1. When do your ribs protect your chest?

   _____

   _____

2. What do your ribs guard?

   _____

3. What guards your chest?

   _____

4. Is your chest protected by bones?

   _____

5. Is your chest protected by your ribs?

   _____

A DEFINITIONS

Write a word that comes from **protect** in each blank.

1. The cop was _____ the shop.

2. That lock will _____ my desk.

3. Those socks had _____ his feet.

4. These big ants are _____ their hill.

5. Ron had a cap to _____ his head.

B FOLLOWING DIRECTIONS

Follow the directions.

1. Write a big **T** in the box.

2. Draw a slanted line from the bottom of the vertical line to the right end of the horizontal line.

3. Draw a slanted line from the left end of the horizontal line to the bottom of the vertical line.

C PARTS OF SPEECH

Underline each part that names. Then circle the noun in that part.

1. The meeting lasted a long time.

2. My mother has a new dress.

3. That tired black horse is very old.

4. Her dad worked very hard.

5. That dream was a nightmare.

6. Jill painted a beautiful picture.

7. This happy baby smiles a lot.

8. Trucks can't drive on this street.

FACT GAME SCORECARD

1	2	3	4	5	6	7	8	9	10	11	12	13	14	15
16	17	18	19	20	21	22	23	24	25	26	27	28	29	30

FG   B   T

Fact Game

1

2. Name the class for each object.

   a. boat
   b. jar
   c. bicycle
   d. bag
   e. truck

3. Say each sentence using another word for the underlined part.

   a. The dog <u>guarded</u> the yard.
   b. The man will <u>get</u> lumber.

4. Answer the questions.

   a. What's another word for **get?**
   b. What's another word for **choose?**

5. Say each sentence using another word for the underlined part.

   a. The doctor <u>looked at</u> the bone.
   b. She will <u>choose</u> a new dress.

6. Say the whole deduction.

Every car is a vehicle. A convertible is a car.

So, ▆▆▆▆▆▆▆.

7. Read the sentence and answer the questions.

A small red car stopped at the corner.
   a. What's the part that names?
   b. What's the noun in that part?

8. Name the bone shown by each letter in the picture.

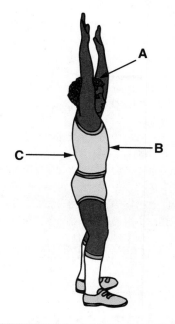

9. Say the whole deduction.

Some bones are long. An ulna is a bone.

So, ▆▆▆▆▆▆.

10. Name the class for each object.

   a. box
   b. car
   c. train
   d. cup
   e. bottle

11. Name the body system of bones.

12. Answer the questions.

   a. What's another word for **guard?**
   b. What's another word for **look at?**

Lesson 6

A DEFINITIONS

Write a word that comes from **examine** in each blank.

1. A dentist will _____ my teeth.

2. That doctor had _____ Tim's ribs.

3. Six cops are _____ that old lock.

4. This vet wants to _____ Barbara's pet.

5. A cook will have to _____ this ham.

B PARTS OF SPEECH

Underline each part that names. Then circle the verbs.

1. Mark worked all morning.

2. Her uncle drove an old car.

3. Her uncle was driving an old car.

4. Her uncle was painting the car.

5. That boy painted a house.

6. My brother was sitting in the kitchen.

7. Doris went to the kitchen.

8. The bus slid on the ice.

C BODY OF SYSTEMS

Write **ribs, skull,** or **spine** in each blank.

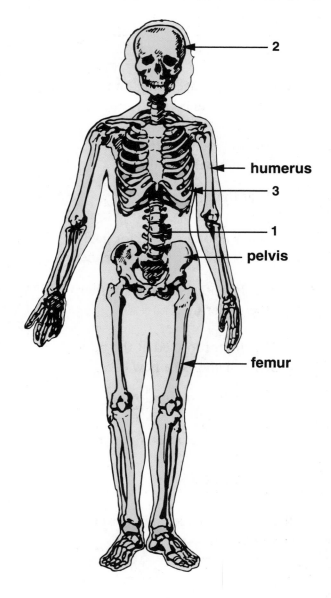

1. _____

2. _____

3. _____

D EVIDENCE

Write the letter of the fact that explains why each thing happened.

> A. Rose eats bananas.
> B. Rose eats ham.

1. She eats things with a peel. _____

2. She eats things that are yellow. _____

3. She eats food that comes from a pig. _____

4. She eats things that are plants. _____

E FOLLOWING DIRECTIONS

Follow the directions.

1. Draw a vertical line in the box.

2. Draw a line that slants up to the right from the bottom of the vertical line.

3. Draw a line that slants up to the left from the bottom of the vertical line.

F INFERENCE

Read the story and answer the questions.

> Pam wanted to swim. She walked to the pond, but a pig was in the pond. She did not want to be seen with a pig, so she ran to the pool.

1. What was in the pond?

_____

2. What did Pam want to do?

_____

3. What did Pam not want to do?

_____

_____

4. Where did Pam walk?

_____

5. How did Pam get to the pool?

_____

A DEFINITIONS

Write a word that comes from **obtain** in each blank.

1. She is _____ a bottle of water.

2. Len wants to _____ a mop from this store.

3. He has _____ a mitt from this store.

4. They are _____ tin and copper from this mine.

5. Sam has _____ red socks for his feet.

B PARTS OF SPEECH

In each part that names, circle the noun. In each sentence, make a box around the verb.

1. The class was making a chart.

2. The class bought large sheets of paper.

3. Six boys were climbing that hill.

4. A black dog crawled under the fence.

5. The girls ran in the park.

6. My sister is running in the park.

7. This train stops every ten minutes.

8. Henry is fixing his bike.

C BODY SYSTEMS

Write **femur, humerus,** or **pelvis** in each blank.

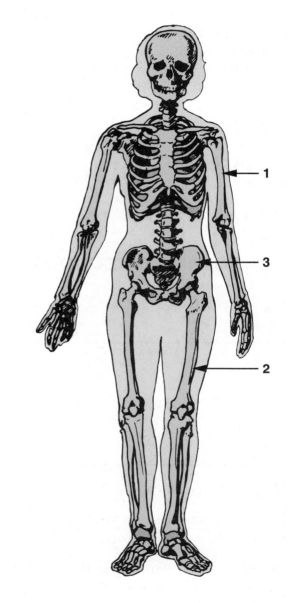

1. _____

2. _____

3. _____

A PARTS OF SPEECH

In each part that names, circle the noun. In each sentence, make a box around the verb.

1. Dan flew a kite.

2. Many birds were drinking from the pond.

3. Her brother slipped on the ice.

4. Three large yellow birds were peeking at Tim.

5. That boy eats all the time.

6. Their mother is making a chair.

7. Tina sold some of her books.

8. Our class went to the lake.

B DEFINITIONS

Write a word that comes from **construct** in each blank.

1. Her dad wants to _____ a home.

2. Those men are planning to

_____ a ship.

3. Her mom is _____ a shed.

4. That man has _____ a tin bathtub.

5. You cannot _____ a ship with sand.

C CLASSIFICATION

Circle each container. Underline each plant. Cross out each animal.

D EVIDENCE

Write the letter of the fact that explains why each thing happened.

> **A.** Dot was sick.
> **B.** Deb was feeling fit.

1. She was sneezing. _____

2. She had a box of pills. _____

3. She ran down the street. _____

4. She went for a swim. _____

E BODY SYSTEMS

Write **femur, humerus, pelvis, ribs, skull,** or **spine** in each blank.

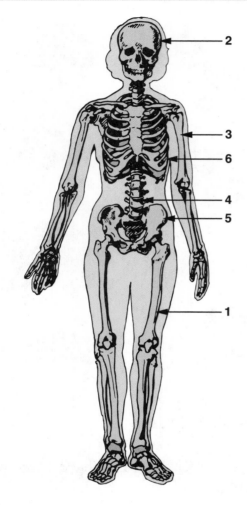

1. _____
2. _____
3. _____
4. _____
5. _____
6. _____

F FOLLOWING DIRECTIONS

Follow the directions.

1. Write an X in the box.
2. Draw three vertical lines to the left of the X.
3. Draw a line from the bottom of a vertical line to the X.

G INFERENCE

Read the story and answer the questions.

A slim man went to a shop. He obtained six gold rings at the shop. He said, "I need to protect these rings. I will lock four in my home and keep the rest in a box."

1. What kind of man went to a shop?

_____

2. What kind of rings did the man get?

_____

3. Why will the man lock some rings in his home?

_____

4. How many rings will he keep in a box?

_____

5. How many rings will he lock in his home?

_____

A PARTS OF SPEECH

In each part that names, circle the noun. In each sentence, make a box around the verb.

1. The weather was very hot.

2. My grandmother is happy.

3. This problem is hard.

4. This problem had three parts.

5. Mary had a pet dog.

6. Ted was running with the dog.

7. Ted was fifteen years old.

8. That truck was carrying fruit.

B DEFINITIONS

Write a word that comes from **select** in each blank.

1. Bill has _____ a lock for his home.

2. Sandra will _____ a lamp for her desk.

3. Ron was _____ by the team.

4. The man is _____ pants at the shop.

5. Tim has to _____ a vet for his dog.

C CLASSIFICATION

Make a line over each vehicle. Circle each food item. Underline each piece of clothing.

D EVIDENCE

Write the letter of the fact that explains why each thing happened.

| A. Jim said, "Sell." |
| B. Bob said, "Cat." |

1. He said a verb. _____

2. He said a noun. _____

3. He named a type of pet. _____

4. He named a type of action. _____

E BODY SYSTEMS

Fill in each blank.

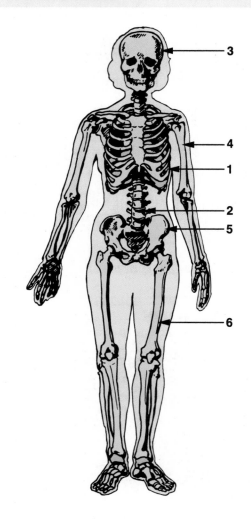

1. _____

2. _____

3. _____

4. _____

5. _____

6. _____

A PARTS OF SPEECH

In each part that names, circle the noun. In each sentence, make a box around the verb.

1. The boy was walking in the yard.

2. The boys were walking in the yard.

3. The boys were in the yard.

4. The boys had a large yard.

5. This day is very warm.

6. Yesterday was hotter.

7. The street feels warm.

8. His mother was going home.

9. His sister carried a large bag.

B PARTS OF SPEECH

Underline both nouns in each sentence.

1. The girl ran to the store.

2. My mother sat under that tree.

3. The man ate the sandwich quickly.

4. Doris read the book very slowly.

5. My brother loves Doris.

6. Many people live in Chicago.

7. Five cats slept in the sun.

8. Sam rode carefully through the gravel.

C DEFINITIONS

Write a word that comes from **protect** in each blank.

1. The mitt is _____ his hand.

2. That shop was _____ by a dog.

3. Your ribs _____ your chest.

4. Your chest is _____ by your ribs.

5. The tree was _____ us from the wind.

D CLASSIFICATION

Circle each tool.
Cross out each living thing.
Underline each piece of clothing.

E BODY SYSTEMS

Fill in each blank.

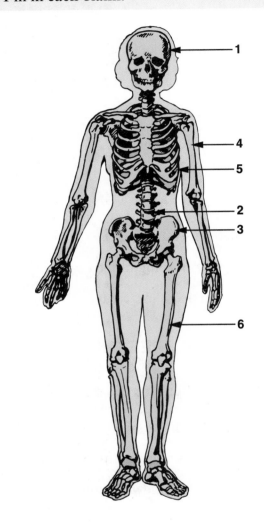

1. _____

2. _____

3. _____

4. _____

5. _____

6. _____

F EVIDENCE

Write the letter of the fact that explains why each thing happened.

> **A.** Jill has mittens.
> **B.** Barb has socks.

1. She has them on her feet. _____

2. They are next to her shirt. _____

3. They are next to her pants. _____

4. She has them on her hands. _____

G FOLLOWING DIRECTIONS

Follow the directions.

1. Draw a vertical line.

2. Draw a line that slants down to the left from the top of the vertical line.

3. Draw a line from the bottom of the slanted line to the bottom of the vertical line.

H INFERENCE

Read the story and answer the questions.

> Bill did not know that bones grow. His dad said, "You are a kid. Your bones grow when you are a kid. That's why you get taller. Your bones don't stop growing until your late teens, when you are as tall as you will be. Your bones will keep growing for seven more years."

1. Bill's dad is 36. Are his bones still growing?

2. If Bill stops growing when he is 19, how old is he now?

3. When do your bones grow?

4. Will Bill's spine grow?

5. Why do you get taller?

6. When are you as tall as you will be?

ERRORS	G	W	B	T

A PARTS OF SPEECH

Underline each noun.

1. The dog chased a ball under the table. (3)

2. Kim put a bag in her car. (3)

3. Tim and Doris did their homework. (3)

4. Cats and dogs had a terrible fight. (3)

5. A little boy crawled under the table. (2)

6. My sister hid her money in a jar. (3)

7. Tim likes Kim better than Sidney. (3)

8. My dad was mowing the lawn. (2)

B INFERENCE

Read the sentences and answer the questions.

- Circle the **W** if the question is answered by words in the sentences. Then underline those words.
- Circle the **D** if the question is answered by a deduction.

> Every person has a spine.
> Don is a person.

1. What does every person have?

   _____ **W** **D**

2. Does Don have a spine?

   _____ **W** **D**

3. Does Don have a bone?

   _____ **W** **D**

4. What is Don?

   _____ **W** **D**

C BODY SYSTEMS

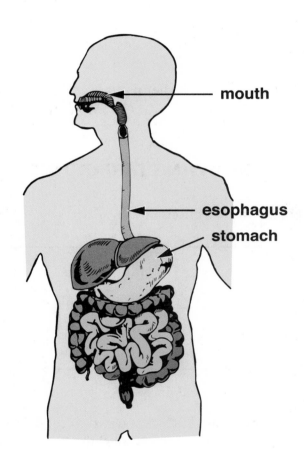

mouth

esophagus

stomach

D PARTS OF SPEECH

Underline the nouns and circle the verbs.

1. The old lion was sleeping. (1)

2. Tim bought new shoes. (2)

3. His old shoes were lying under the bed. (2)

4. Our city built a park and a road. (3)

5. Marvin laughed. (1)

6. The car had a bent door. (2)

7. Six boys and two dogs ran along the beach. (3)

E FOLLOWING DIRECTIONS

Fill in each blank. Then do what the sentence tells you to do.

_____	_____	_____
glip	t	dup

_____	_____	_____ .
m	yek	zork

dup—circle
glip—make
m—on
t—a
yek—the
zork—line

_____

F DEFINITIONS

Write a word that comes from **examine** in each blank.

1. That doctor has _____ my spine.

2. That doctor will now _____ her femur.

3. Ten kids are _____ this lock.

4. A shopper wants to _____ an old dress.

5. His dog's spine was _____ by a vet.

G DEDUCTIONS

Complete the deductions.

1. Every person has a skull.
   John is a person.

   _____

2. Some animals have bones.
   Snakes are animals.

   _____

3. Insects do not have spines.
   Antelopes are mammals.

   _____

4. John has every kind of bone.
   Ribs are bones.

   _____

Lesson 11

H BODY SYSTEMS

Fill in each blank.

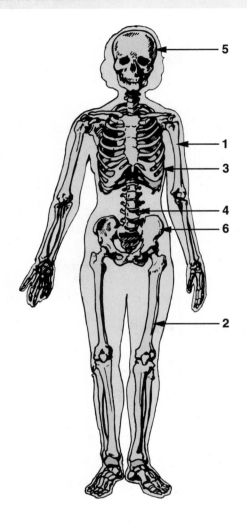

1. _____
2. _____
3. _____
4. _____
5. _____
6. _____

E FOLLOWING DIRECTIONS

Fill in each blank. Then do what the sentence tells you to do.

_____   _____   _____
glaf   ag   preb

_____   _____   _____
rop   k   wid

_____.
hux

ag—the
glaf—write
hux—line
k—on
preb—word
rop—man
wid—the

_____

F EVIDENCE

Write the letter of the fact that explains why each thing happened.

| A. Ann has holes in her teeth. |
| B. Pat has a crack in her humerus. |

1. She has to see a bone doctor. _____

2. She has to get fillings. _____

3. She has to get a cast. _____

4. She has to see a dentist. _____

G BODY SYSTEMS

Fill in each blank.

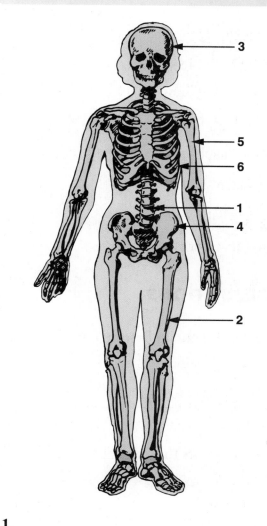

1. _____

2. _____

3. _____

4. _____

5. _____

6. _____

A PARTS OF SPEECH

Draw a line over each adjective.

1. Six cats played.

2. That dog jumped.

3. That big dog jumped.

4. A big dog jumped.

5. An old black cat ran.

6. Ten sheep slept.

7. Six men sat.

8. A red truck crashed.

B DEFINITIONS

Write a word that comes from **obtain** in each blank.

1. The robber will _____ a robe for his back.

2. The ram wants to _____ some oats to eat.

3. The man has _____ a pig for a pet.

4. Six shoppers are _____ ten socks.

5. Ten socks were _____ by six shoppers.

C INFERENCE

Read the sentences and answer the questions.

- Circle the **W** if the question is answered by words in the sentences. Then underline those words.
- Circle the **D** if the question is answered by a deduction.

Cristina does not like vehicles. Cristina does not have any animals.

1. Does Cristina have a cat?

_____ **W D**

2. What does Cristina not like?

_____ **W D**

3. Does Cristina like trucks?

_____ **W D**

4. Who doesn't have any animals?

_____ **W D**

D BODY SYSTEMS

Write **esophagus, mouth,** or **stomach** in each blank.

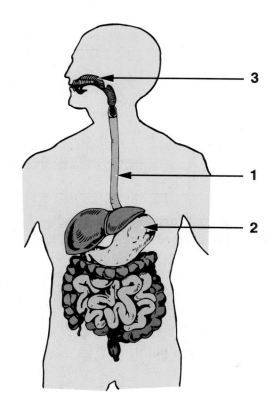

1. _____

2. _____

3. _____

E FOLLOWING DIRECTIONS

Fill in each blank. Then do what the sentence tells you to do.

_____	_____	_____
zup	om	jek
_____	_____	_____.
des	v	frab

des—in
frab—box
jek—R
om—an
v—the
zup—write

F EVIDENCE

Write the letter of the fact that explains why each thing happened.

> **A.** A robin is a bird.
> **B.** A perch is a fish.

1. It lives in a pond. _____

2. It has a nest. _____

3. It lives in a tree. _____

4. It swims and swims. _____

G PARTS OF SPEECH

Circle the verbs. Underline the nouns.

1. His mom constructed a shed.

2. His mom has constructed that shed.

3. Six men will obtain ten socks.

4. The shoppers will be shopping for hats.

5. A man was mopping with a mop.

6. Three men are mopping floors with mops.

7. A metal ship is rocking in the deep pond.

8. That shop has sold hats and socks.

H DEDUCTIONS

Complete the deductions.

1. Linda did not have any containers.
   A jar is a container.

   _____

   _____

2. Most men have 206 bones.
   Jim is a man.

   _____

   _____

3. Some objects are made by hand.
   That cup is an object.

   _____

   _____

4. Every plant is a living thing.
   A tern is not a plant.

   _____

D PARTS OF SPEECH

Circle the verbs. Underline the nouns.

1. That man will crack a big bone.

2. Some animals drink.

3. Six rabbits jumped over a bench.

4. Ten sheep jumped on a wall.

5. Ten sheep and six rabbits are hopping on bricks.

6. This small boy has made a big hop.

7. His mom and dad are walking.

8. His pal constructs boxes.

E DEDUCTIONS

Complete the deductions.

1. Bill had some plants. A weed is a plant.

   _____

   _____

2. Every noun names a person, place, or thing. **Protective** is an adjective.

   _____

   _____

3. Verbs do not name a place. **Sing** is a verb.

   _____

   _____

4. Some words have many forms. **Verbs** are words.

   _____

   _____

F BODY SYSTEMS

Fill in each blank.

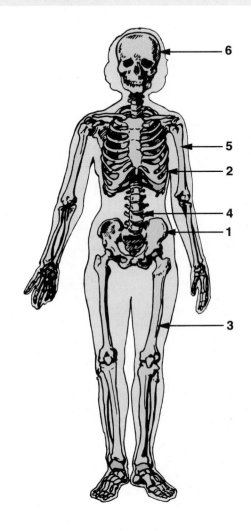

1. _____

2. _____

3. _____

4. _____

5. _____

6. _____

G FOLLOWING DIRECTIONS

Fill in each blank. Then do what the sentence tells you to do.

_____	_____	_____
gluk	rik	bip

_____	_____	_____.
fud	fim	weg

bip—X
fim—a
fud—in
gluk—make
rik—an
weg—box

H BODY SYSTEMS

Write **esophagus, mouth,** or **stomach** in each blank.

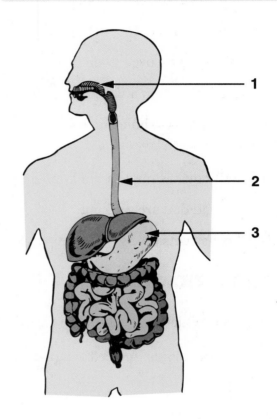

1. _____

2. _____

3. _____

I FOLLOWING DIRECTIONS

Follow the directions.

1. Draw a big circle in the box.

2. Draw a line from the top of the circle to the bottom of the circle.

3. Shade the part of the circle that is to the right of the line.

4. Draw a box in the part of the circle that is to the left of the line.

J EVIDENCE

Write the letter of the fact that explains why each thing happened.

> **A.** Goats give milk.
> **B.** Goats eat many kinds of plants.

1. The goat owner did not buy milk at the store. _____

2. The goat owner never mowed her lawn. _____

3. The goat owner made butter at home. _____

4. The goat ate green food that grew in the ground. _____

WORD LIST

adjective (n) a word that comes before a noun and tells about the noun

digestive system (n) the body system that changes food into fuel for the body

esophagus (n) the tube that goes from the mouth to the stomach

femur (n) the upper leg bone

humerus (n) the upper arm bone

mouth (n) the body part that takes solid and liquid food into the body

noun (n) a word that names a person, place, or thing

pelvis (n) the hip bone

protect (v) to guard

protection (n) something that protects

protective (a) that something protects

stomach (n) the organ that mixes food with chemicals

verb (n) a word that tells the action that things do

A BODY SYSTEMS

Write **esophagus, mouth,** or **stomach** in each blank.

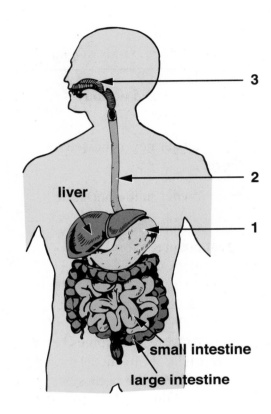

liver

3

2

1

small intestine

large intestine

1. _____

2. _____

3. _____

B PARTS OF SPEECH

Draw a line over each adjective.

1. That <u>man</u> was running a <u>show</u>.

2. His <u>brother</u> was running a big <u>show</u>.

3. My <u>uncle</u> was running that <u>show</u>.

4. Four fat <u>cats</u> were running near a deep <u>lake</u>.

5. Her <u>cat</u> was sitting under a green <u>tree</u>.

6. A <u>man</u> ate six red <u>plums</u>.

7. That <u>man</u> was sitting on red <u>plants</u>.

8. Some <u>ants</u> were eating the <u>plants</u>.

C ANALOGIES

Complete the analogy.

A bird is to flying

1. as a fish is to _____ ,

2. as a frog is to _____ ,

3. as a horse is to _____ .

D DEFINITIONS

Fill in each blank with the word that has the same meaning as the word or words under the blank.

1. He told her to _____ six locks.
   (choose)

2. A cat is _____ that tree.
   (looking at)

3. That shed was not _____ by her dad.
   (built)

4. Those trees are _____ these crops.
   (guarding)

E INFERENCE

Read the sentences and answer the questions.

- Circle the **W** if the question is answered by words in the sentences. Then underline those words.
- Circle the **D** if the question is answered by a deduction.

Pam is shorter than Lara. Lara is thinner than Pam.

1. Which person is shorter?

   _____ W   D

2. Which person is taller?

   _____ W   D

3. Which person is thinner?

   _____ W   D

4. Which person is fatter?

   _____ W   D

F PARTS OF SPEECH

Circle the verbs and underline the nouns.

1. Broken bones need casts.

2. Six girls went to the store.

3. Six girls and six dogs went to the well.

4. His dad is going to a show.

5. Clowns showed that man a hat.

6. The woman dug holes.

7. The woman dug holes and pits.

G DEDUCTIONS

Complete the deductions.

1. Some animals drink milk.
   A fish is an animal.

   _____

   _____

2. Fred has every kind of tool. Milk is food.

   _____

   _____

3. Every person has a skeletal system.
   Sam is a deer.

   _____

   _____

4. Pam did not have any vehicles.
   A bike is a vehicle.

   _____

   _____

H FOLLOWING DIRECTIONS

Fill in each blank. Then do what the sentence tells you to do.

_____ _____ _____
     76   89   54

_____ _____.
     23   45

23—left
45—circle
54—the
76—shade
89—in

I FOLLOWING DIRECTIONS

Follow the directions.

1. Draw a big square.

2. Draw a slanted line from the bottom left corner to the top right corner of the square.

3. Shade the part of the square that is under the slanted line.

4. Draw a slanted line from the top left corner to the bottom right corner of the square.

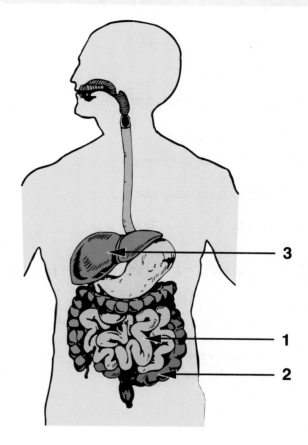
A PARTS OF SPEECH

Draw a line over each adjective.

1. Plants need sunlight.
2. Some plants need bright sunlight.
3. The workers were fixing streets.
4. Henry was sitting in a small truck.
5. His big dog ran near town.
6. The girl sat in a red boat.
7. Five red ants walked under the bench.
8. Those ants walked to the store.
9. Ants run under rugs.
10. Black smoke came from the stove.
11. My teacher was reading from a green book.

B BODY SYSTEMS

Write **liver, large intestine,** or **small intestine** in each blank.

3
1
2

1. _____

2. _____

3. _____

C SENTENCE COMBINATIONS

Put the correct end mark on each sentence.

1. The man went to the store
2. Where did the man go
3. What did you do
4. Those kids are playing
5. Whose kid is that
6. When will we go home
7. Her mom sat on a log
8. Bob and Ellen ate figs

D SENTENCE COMBINATIONS

Underline the common part.

1. Tom had a bike.
   Tom ate beans.

2. Tom had a bike.
   Bob had a bike.

3. His mom went home.
   His mom ate meat.

4. Linda and Anna drink milk.
   Those men drink milk.

5. Six old dogs dug holes.
   Six old dogs sat down.

6. That plane is fast.
   This truck is fast.

7. The man was eating.
   The man was drinking.

E INFERENCE

Read the story and answer the questions.
- Circle the **W** if the question is answered by words in the story. Then underline those words.
- Circle the **D** if the question is answered by a deduction.

It was summer, and Linda did not have anything to do. She said to herself, "Life is too boring. The less you have to do, the more boring life gets. I have to think of something to do." She tried to think of things to do, but nothing seemed like fun. At last, she said, "I think I will play a team sport."

1. What time of year was it?

   _____ **W D**

2. Did this happen in November?

   _____ **W D**

3. When does life get more boring?

   _____

   _____ **W D**

4. If Linda has less to do on Monday than on Sunday, which day is more boring?

   _____ **W D**

5. What kind of sport will Linda play?

   _____ **W D**

6. Name three team sports.

   _____

   _____

   _____ **W D**

F ANALOGIES

Complete the analogy.

A nose is to smelling

1. as eyes are to _____,

2. as ears are to _____,

3. as feet are to _____.

G DEFINITIONS

Fill in each blank with the word that has the same meaning as the word or words under the blank.

1. She _____ some pants
for herself. (got)

2. A farmer _____ a shed
for her pigs. (built)

3. A dog was picked to _____
the shed. (guard)

4. They are _____ a home
to live in. (choosing)

H PARTS OF SPEECH

Circle the verbs and underline the nouns.

1. A dog was panting.

2. His mother was opening a box.

3. His mom opened boxes.

4. His mom opened boxes and closed boxes.

5. Her pal constructs boxes and paints rocks.

6. A man was drinking water and sitting in a truck.

7. An old fish and a frog are swimming.

I DEDUCTIONS

Complete the deductions.

1. Every fish has gills. A carp is a fish.

_____

_____

2. Most living things do not have bones. A crab is a living thing.

_____

_____

3. Dan had 206 bones. A bike is a vehicle.

_____

_____

4. Rocks are not plants. Gold is a rock.

_____

_____

A PARTS OF SPEECH

Draw a line over each adjective.

1. Her <u>dad</u> lifted that <u>log</u>.

2. <u>Workers</u> sat on a thick <u>log</u>.

3. A <u>man</u> jumped over an old <u>log</u>.

4. His <u>dad</u> ate <u>apples</u>.

5. This slim <u>cat</u> examined small <u>trees</u>.

6. The <u>cat</u> ran to those <u>trees</u>.

7. His <u>dog</u> sat under that <u>log</u>.

8. That <u>deer</u> has jumped over ten <u>logs</u>.

B SENTENCE COMBINATIONS

Make each sentence begin with a capital letter. Put the correct end mark on each sentence.

1. the pelvis is the hip bone

2. which bone is the backbone

3. that plant is green

4. how will you get home

5. where is the femur

6. ten frogs hopped over those logs

C SENTENCE COMBINATIONS

Underline the common part. Then combine the sentences with **and.**

1. Marco had bags.
   Marco had cups.

   _____

   _____

2. Linda went to the store.
   Linda got six mats.

   _____

   _____

3. Ten bees bit a camper.
   Ten bees bit three dogs.

   _____

   _____

4. A dog protected the store.
   A dog chomped on a bone.

   _____

   _____

   _____

5. His dad broke a dish.
   His dad broke some glasses.

   _____

   _____

D ANALOGIES

Complete the analogy.

Protect is to **guard**

1. as **select** is to _____,

2. as **obtain** is to _____,

3. as **construct** is to _____.

E DEFINITIONS

Write a word that comes from **select** in each blank. Then write **verb, noun,** or **adjective** after each item.

1. Pam has _____ two dresses at the shop. _____

2. His mom was a _____ shopper. _____

3. The shop had a wide _____ of bottles. _____

4. They laughed at our _____ of hats. _____

5. That girl will _____ wheels for her truck. _____

F INFERENCE

Read the story and answer the questions.
- Circle the **W** if the question is answered by words in the story. Then underline those words.
- Circle the **D** if the question is answered by a deduction.

Linda did not know what team sport to play. She said to herself, "My brother broke a rib playing football, and my sister broke her humerus playing basketball. I don't think I'll play those sports. But if I play baseball, I won't get hurt and I can play on the park team." So, she went to a sports store to select a bat.

1. What did Linda's brother break?

_____ W D

2. Where was the bone Linda's sister broke?

_____

_____ W D

3. Linda's sister and brother both hurt the same body system. What's the name of that system?

_____

4. What won't happen to Linda if she plays baseball?

_____

5. Why did Linda go to a sports store?

_____ W D

6. How many things will she select at the sports store?

_____ W D

G PARTS OF SPEECH

Circle the verbs and underline the nouns.

1. That cat was sitting in a tree.

2. That cat was in a tree.

3. That man was a cop.

4. Those men were cops.

5. Those men were running.

6. Six dogs are running to the beach.

7. Six dogs are on the beach.

8. Six dogs have bones.

9. Her cat has run.

10. That cat has a rat.

H DEDUCTIONS

Complete the deductions.

1. Some words are verbs. **Indent** is a word.

   _____

   _____

2. Every bone needs milk. Spines are bones.

   _____

   _____

3. Gene did not have any trucks. A flatbed is a truck.

   _____

   _____

4. Most men wear socks. Bob is a man.

   _____

   _____

I BODY SYSTEMS

Write **esophagus, large intestine, liver, mouth, small intestine,** or **stomach** in each blank.

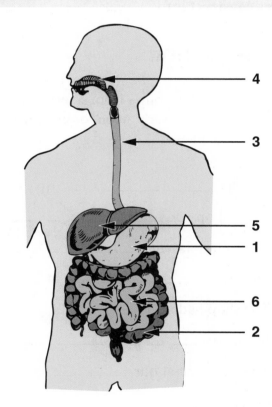

1. _____

2. _____

3. _____

4. _____

5. _____

6. _____

D SENTENCE COMBINATIONS

Underline the common part. Then combine the sentences with **and.**

1. Roz liked to eat chicken.
   Roz liked to drink milk.

   _____

   _____

2. The shop had a sale.
   The shop made lots of money.

   _____

   _____

   _____

3. Bill sold his truck.
   Bill obtained a boat.

   _____

   _____

4. The ram broke the gate.
   The ram ran down the street.

   _____

   _____

   _____

5. Her mom selected ten locks.
   Her mom selected six plates.

   _____

   _____

E PARTS OF SPEECH

Circle the verbs. Underline the nouns.

1. Those objects were bones.

2. Those people were sitting.

3. An object was on the box.

4. His pet went to the creek.

5. His pet has gone to the creek.

6. That frog is in the creek.

7. That frog was hopping.

8. A log will bump that frog.

9. Logs are objects.

10. The dog had a ball.

F EVIDENCE

Write the letter of the fact that explains why each thing happened.

> **A.** Pat said, "Selective."
> **B.** Bill said, "Protection."

1. He said a noun. _____

2. He said an adjective. _____

3. He was talking about
   something that guards. _____

4. He was talking about something
   that is careful about choosing. _____

G PARTS OF SPEECH

Draw a line **over** the adjectives.

1. A rug was blowing in the wind.

2. Three green frogs were jumping.

3. Those red robins were protecting their nest.

4. Robins are digging under trees.

5. Big bugs and big cats were running.

6. Cats have eaten under that bench.

7. Six dogs will eat meat.

8. Ten dogs ate meat and drank cold milk.

H ANALOGIES

Complete the analogy.

Red is to adjective

1. as **pig** is to _____,

2. as **protect** is to _____,

3. as **protective** is to _____.

I BODY SYSTEMS

Fill in each blank.

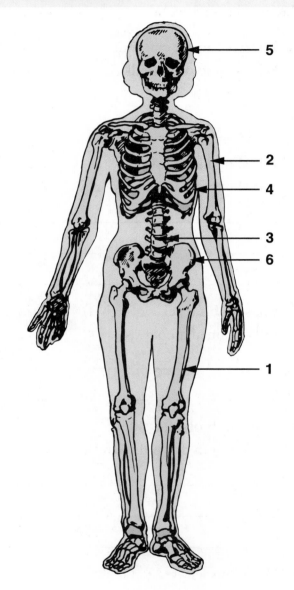

1. _____

2. _____

3. _____

4. _____

5. _____

6. _____

J INFERENCE

Read the story and answer the questions.
- Circle the **W** if the question is answered by words in the story. Then underline those words.
- Circle the **D** if the question is answered by a deduction.

Linda got a baseball bat and walked to the park, where she saw a baseball team and a coach. Linda asked the coach if she could play on the team, but the coach said, "You have to get good at batting before you can play." So Linda asked the coach to help her learn how to bat.

The coach tossed the ball to Linda, and Linda swung at it. The bat went **thud,** and the ball rolled six feet. The coach said, "You have to swing harder. The harder you swing, the farther the ball will go."

---

1. What was the first thing Linda asked the coach?

   _____

   _____ **W**　**D**

2. What was the next thing Linda asked the coach?

   _____

   _____ **W**　**D**

3. What does Linda have to get good at before she can play?

   _____

4. Who tossed the ball to Linda?

   _____

5. How far did Linda hit the ball?

   _____

6. If the coach swings harder than Linda, which person will hit the ball farther?

   _____ **W**　**D**

7. If player A hits the ball 100 feet and player B hits the ball 150 feet, which player swings harder?

   _____ **W**　**D**

K **BODY SYSTEMS**

Fill in each blank.

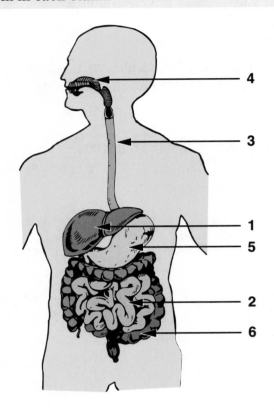

1. _____

2. _____

3. _____

4. _____

5. _____

6. _____

A BODY SYSTEMS

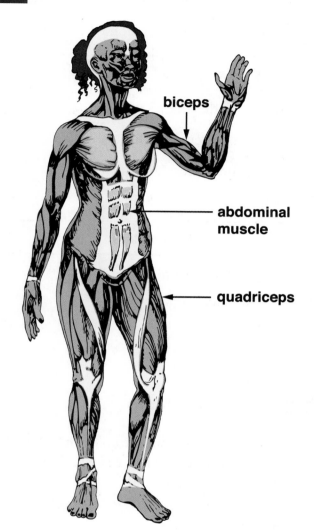

biceps

abdominal muscle

quadriceps

B PARTS OF SPEECH

Underline the nouns. Draw a line **over** the adjectives.

1. His mom constructed a shed. (2)

2. A big bus was in that shed. (2)

3. Ten socks are on that clothesline. (2)

4. The man selected some clothes. (2)

5. Some shoppers are selecting red hats. (2)

6. Cats sat under that protective wall. (2)

7. Those kids and those dogs obtained bananas. (3)

8. These girls examined red trucks and red bikes. (3)

C SENTENCE COMBINATIONS

Correct the sentences.

1. his mom had lots of cash

2. whose mom had cash

3. where will you spend that cash

4. pigs are farm animals

5. why are those hens clucking

6. some cups are made of tin

D SENTENCE COMBINATIONS

Underline the common part. Then combine the sentences with **and.**

1. Jim liked ham.
   Hector liked ham.

   _____

   _____

2. Cristy wanted to swim.
   Deb wanted to swim.

   _____

   _____

3. His cat felt tired.
   Her dog felt tired.

   _____

   _____

4. The woman jumped into bed.
   The woman went to sleep.

   _____

   _____

   _____

5. Her dad seemed sad.
   His mom seemed sad.

   _____

   _____

6. Greg sat on a gate.
   Greg fell down.

   _____

   _____

E CONTRADICTIONS

Underline each contradiction.

Sam is taller than Bill.

1. Bill is shorter than Sam.

2. Sam is shorter than Bill.

3. Sam is not taller than Bill.

4. Bill is not as tall as Sam.

All birds have only two legs.

5. Only some birds have two legs.

6. All birds have three legs.

7. Every bird has two legs.

8. No birds have two legs.

F DEFINITIONS

Write a word that comes from **examine** or **select** in each blank. Then write **verb, noun,** or **adjective** after each item.

1. A doctor will _____

   Kim's teeth. _____

2. The coach made three _____

   for the team. _____

3. Some vets do not _____

   big animals. _____

4. His sister is a very _____

   person. _____

5. Bob had a big _____

   of CDs. _____

G DEDUCTIONS

Use the rule to answer the questions.

> The faster you run, the faster your heart beats.

1. Lucy and Maria are running. Lucy's heart is beating 90 times a minute. Maria's heart is beating 70 times a minute.
   a. Which girl is running faster?

   _____

   b. How do you know?

   _____

   _____

2. Dolly ran six miles in one hour. Bob ran nine miles in one hour.
   a. Whose heart beat faster?

   _____

   b. How do you know?

   _____

   _____

3. Karen and Pam had a race from the school to the construction site. Karen finished in 20 minutes. Pam finished in 15 minutes.
   a. Which person's heart beat faster?

   _____

   b. How do you know?

   _____

   _____

H PARTS OF SPEECH

Circle the verbs. Underline the nouns.

1. A boat was in the dock.
2. Her dog runs and pants.
3. His pants were in the washer.
4. That washer was washing clothes.
5. This wall gave good protection from robbers.
6. The men protected their gold.
7. Those girls have constructed a home.
8. Those women were teachers.

I ANALOGIES

Complete the analogy.

> A femur is to a leg

1. as a humerus is to an _____,
2. as a spine is to a _____,
3. as a pelvis is to a _____.

J **INFERENCE**

Read the story and answer the questions.
- Circle the **W** if the question is answered by words in the story. Then underline those words.
- Circle the **D** if the question is answered by a deduction.

The coach was teaching Linda how to hit a baseball. Linda tried to swing the bat harder, but the ball did not go much farther. The coach said, "When you swing a bat, you have to use your arms. The stronger your arms, the harder you swing. You need to make your arm muscles stronger. You can make them stronger by swinging bats and lifting barbells." So Linda walked home and started to work on her arm muscles.

---

1. What happened when Linda tried to swing harder?

   _____

   _____ **W**   **D**

2. What will Linda be able to do if she makes her arm muscles stronger?

   _____

3. How can Linda make her arm muscles stronger?

   _____

   _____ **W**   **D**

4. What is the name of one muscle that Linda needs to make stronger?

   _____ **W**   **D**

5. The coach can swing harder than Linda. Which one has stronger arms?

   _____ **W**   **D**

6. How did Linda get home?

   _____

A DEFINITIONS

Write a word that comes from **construct** in each blank. Then write **verb, noun,** or **adjective** after each item.

1. The farmer is _____

   a pen for goats. _____

2. Some _____ are

   made of metal. _____

3. Students like that _____

   teacher. _____

4. Last year his mother _____

   a gate for the yard. _____

5. This _____ book will

   teach you how to read. _____

B PARTS OF SPEECH

Underline the nouns. Draw a line **over** the adjectives.

1. A brass band will play in the town. (2)

2. His dad and his sister were sitting on logs. (3)

3. The man drove his car down the street. (3)

4. That car is on the wide street. (2)

5. Five dogs ate red meat and brown wheat. (3)

6. Her pal ate in the shed. (2)

7. His sister ate in shacks. (2)

8. A green box is on that bench. (2)

C SENTENCE COMBINATIONS

Underline the common part. Then combine the sentences with **and.**

1. Sheets are white. Sheep are white.

   _____

   _____

2. Six cups were on the stove.
   Three plates were on the stove.

   _____

   _____

   _____

3. Men eat fish. Cats eat fish.

   _____

   _____

4. Sid bit his lip. Sid wiped his nose.

   _____

   _____

5. A man constructed that shed.
   A man constructed this porch.

   _____

   _____

   _____

6. Jill wanted to see the gold.
   Linda wanted to see the gold.

   _____

   _____

D CONTRADICTIONS

Underline each contradiction.

| The ribs are in the skeletal system. |

1. The ribs are in the digestive system.
2. The ribs are in the system of bones.
3. The ribs are in the system of muscles.
4. The ribs are bones.

| Sharon is faster than Linda. |

5. Linda is not as fast as Sharon.
6. Linda is faster than Sharon.
7. Sharon is slower than Linda.
8. Linda is slower than Sharon.

E PARTS OF SPEECH

Circle the verbs. Underline the nouns.

1. Those five old men sip milk.
2. Fleas like his dog.
3. The sad student was weeping.
4. Her brother was a champ.
5. Her brother and his mom were champs.
6. Campers were eating corn and drinking milk.
7. A protective mat covered the shelf.
8. Ten goats and six pigs rolled in the mud.

F ANALOGIES

Complete the analogy.

| A sack is to containers |

1. as a cat is to _____

   _____ ,

2. as trees are to _____

   _____ ,

3. as a ship is to _____ .

G DEDUCTIONS

Use the rule to answer the questions.

| The hotter the air, the more water it can hold. |

1. Air in a stove is hotter than air in a freezer.
   a. Which air can hold more water?

   _____

   b. How do you know?

   _____

   _____

2. Summer air can hold more water than winter air.
   a. Which air is hotter?

   _____

   b. How do you know?

   _____

   _____

3. The air in the cave is colder than the air on the hill.

a. Which air can hold more water?

_____

b. How do you know?

_____

_____

I BODY SYSTEMS

Fill in each blank.

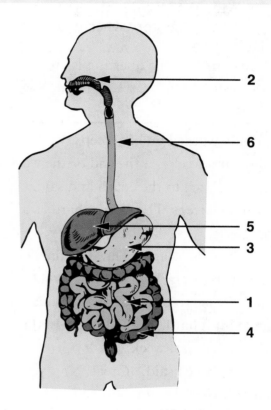

H FOLLOWING DIRECTIONS

Follow the directions.

1. Print a large **L** in the box.

2. Write the word **adjective** below the horizontal line.

3. Write the word **noun** above the vertical line.

1. _____

2. _____

3. _____

4. _____

5. _____

6. _____

J **INFERENCE**

Read the story and answer the questions.
- Circle the **W** if the question is answered by words in the story. Then underline those words.
- Circle the **D** if the question is answered by a deduction.

> Linda worked on her biceps two hours a day for a week. At the end of the week, she went back to the coach and said, "Feel my biceps. They are as hard as a rock."
>
> The coach said, "They feel fine. Let's see how much farther you can hit the ball." So she tossed the ball to Linda, and Linda hit it hard. The ball went 10 times farther than last week.
>
> The coach said, "Great! Now you can play on the team." Linda was happy.

1. Which muscles did Linda work on?

   _____ **W** **D**

2. Where are those muscles located?

   _____

   _____ **W** **D**

3. Linda worked on her muscles for a week. So how many days did she work on her muscles?

   _____ **W** **D**

4. Linda worked on her muscles for two hours a day. So how many hours did she work on her muscles during the whole week?

   _____ **W** **D**

5. How many times farther did the ball go than last week?

   _____ **W** **D**

6. Last week Linda hit the ball six feet. So how many feet did she hit it this week?

   _____ **W** **D**

7. Why was Linda happy?

   _____

   _____

   _____

   _____

   _____

A WRITING DIRECTIONS

Complete the instructions.

②   ③

skull _____ **ribs**

①

1. Draw a _____ line.

2. Write the word _____ on the

   _____ end of the line.

3. Write the word _____ on the

   _____ end of the line.

B ANALOGIES

Complete the analogies.

1. **Tell how each animal moves.**

   A fish is to _____

   as a bird is to _____ .

2. **Tell what parts each animal moves with.**

   A fish is to _____

   as a bird is to _____ .

3. **Tell where you find each animal.**

   A fish is to _____

   as a bird is to _____ .

C SENTENCE COMBINATIONS

Underline the common part. Then combine the sentences with **and.**

1. John jumps.
   Mara jumps.

   _____

2. Jim drinks milk.
   Billie drinks milk.

   _____

   _____

3. That horse eats grass.
   This goat eats grass.

   _____

   _____

4. His dad liked the town.
   Her brother liked the town.

   _____

   _____

   _____

5. The cat hopped over the gate.
   The cat ran down the street.

   _____

   _____

   _____

6. Kangaroos have fur.
   Goats have fur.

   _____

   _____

D CONTRADICTIONS

Underline each contradiction.

> Every bone needs milk.

1. A femur does not need milk.

2. A humerus needs milk.

3. Only some bones need milk.

4. No parts of the skeletal system need milk.

> The biceps is a muscle.

5. The biceps is a bone.

6. The biceps is in the muscular system.

7. The biceps is not in the skeletal system.

8. The biceps is part of the digestive system.

E BODY SYSTEMS

Write **abdominal muscle, biceps,** or **quadriceps** in each blank.

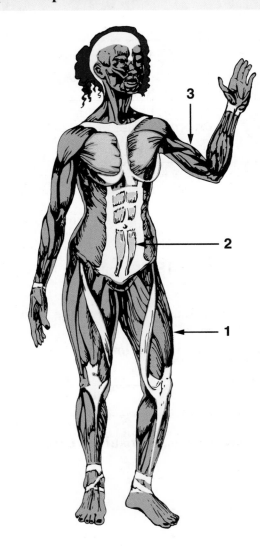

1. _____

2. _____

3. _____

F INFERENCE

Read the story and answer the questions.
- Circle the **W** if the question is answered by words in the story. Then underline those words.
- Circle the **D** if the question is answered by a deduction.

> All foods are made up of things called **nutrients.** There are only six kinds of nutrients: carbohydrates, fats, proteins, vitamins, minerals, and water. If your body doesn't get all six nutrients, it won't work right. If you don't get any minerals, your teeth will rot and your bones will get soft. If you don't get any proteins, your body will get weak and your muscles will shrink.

1. What are all foods made up of?

2. What are the six nutrients?

3. Will your body work right if you don't get any fats? **W   D**

4. If you don't get any minerals, what will happen to your teeth?

5. If Bob never eats any proteins, his muscles will

6. If your bones get soft, what nutrient aren't you getting? **W   D**

G PARTS OF SPEECH

Underline the nouns. Draw a line **over** the adjectives.

1. Every person in the room was eating. (2)
2. Those men were drinking hot drinks. (2)
3. A green car rolled down the steep hill. (2)
4. Five white kites floated in the pond. (2)
5. That kid sails boats. (2)
6. His older sister sat near rocks. (2)
7. Ducks are near big red trees. (2)
8. This car has red seats and a red rug. (3)

H PARTS OF SPEECH

Circle the verbs. Underline the nouns.

1. A big kid planted trees in the forest.
2. Trees are big plants.
3. That man has ten trees.
4. Those crows protected their eggs.
5. The crows protected their eggs and selected these twigs.
6. Animals live in forests and on ranches.
7. My pals were living near the town.
8. Six kangaroos were in the zoo.

I DEDUCTIONS

Use the rule to answer the questions.

> If you don't get any vitamin C, you get a disease called **scurvy.**

1. Bill doesn't get any vitamin C.
   a. What will happen to Bill?

   _____

   _____

   b. How do you know?

   _____

   _____

   _____

2. Pam got scurvy.
   a. What else do you know about Pam?

   _____

   _____

   b. How do you know?

   _____

   _____

3. Mike eats lemons, which have a lot of vitamin C. Fred never eats lemons or any other foods with vitamin C.
   a. Which person will get scurvy?

   _____

   b. How do you know?

   _____

   _____

   _____

J DEFINITIONS

Write a word that comes from **select** in each blank. Then write **verb, noun,** or **adjective** after each item.

1. That coach is _____ players

   for her basketball team. _____

2. The coach had to be very

   _____ because there were

   lots of good players. _____

3. The coach's first _____
   was a tall girl who could rebound.

   _____

4. She made nine more _____

   before she finished. _____

5. "Now I need to _____
   players for my baseball team," she said.

   _____

K EVIDENCE

Write the letter of the fact that explains why each thing happened.

> A. Joe makes predictions about football.
> B. Jack is selective about his CDs.

1. He says that things will happen. _____

2. He chooses tunes carefully. _____

3. He says which team will win. _____

4. He is picky about what he buys. _____

5. Cups are containers.
Plates are containers.

_____

_____

6. Terry felt sick.
Terry went to bed.

_____

_____

E CONTRADICTIONS

Underline each contradiction.

Every body part does a job.

1. The femur does a job.

2. The liver does not do a job.

3. Only some body parts do a job.

4. The ribs and the spine do not do a job.

Only plants and animals are living things.

5. Only plants are living things.

6. A hammer is not a living thing.

7. A cup is a living thing.

8. Only animals are alive.

F INFERENCE

Read the story and answer the questions.
- Circle the **W** if the question is answered by words in the story. Then underline those words.
- Circle the **D** if the question is answered by a deduction.

There are 13 kinds of vitamins: A, C, D, E, K, and 8 B vitamins. Each vitamin does many different things for your body. Vitamin A helps you grow, and it also helps you see better. The B vitamins help keep your muscles strong. Vitamin C is good for your skin and gums. Vitamin D keeps your bones and teeth strong. And vitamin K is good for your blood and liver.

1. What are the 13 kinds of vitamins?

_____ **W   D**

_____

2. If a person can't see well, what vitamin does he or she need?

_____

3. If Linda gets more B vitamins than Maria, whose muscles stay stronger?

_____ **W   D**

4. Which vitamin is good for your spine?

_____

5. Which vitamin helps a part of the digestive system?

_____

6. Which vitamins are good for your biceps?

_____

7. If Bob wants to keep his femurs strong, which vitamin should he take?

_____

G DEDUCTIONS

Complete the deductions.

1. Some adjectives tell what kind of noun. **Abstract** is an adjective.

   _____

   _____

2. Sid has every bone. A pelvis is a bone.

   _____

   _____

3. Insects do not have bones. Ants are insects.

   _____

   _____

H DEDUCTIONS

Use the rule to answer the questions.

If you don't get any vitamin D, your bones get soft.

1. Pam's femur was so soft that it started to bend.
   a. What vitamin wasn't Pam getting?

   _____

   b. How do you know?

   _____

   _____

   _____

2. You can get vitamin D from the sun. Bill goes to the beach every day. Bob always stays in a dark room.
   a. Which person is getting more vitamin D from the sun?

   _____

   b. Which person can get soft bones?

   _____

I BODY SYSTEMS

Write **abdominal muscle, biceps,** or **quadriceps** in each blank.

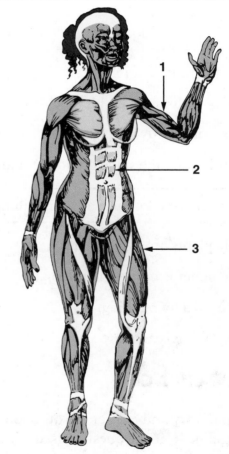

1. _____

2. _____

3. _____

J BODY SYSTEMS

Fill in each blank.

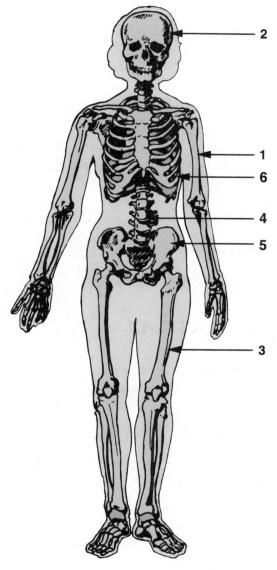

1. _____
2. _____
3. _____
4. _____
5. _____
6. _____

K DEFINITIONS

Fill in each blank with the word that has the same meaning as the word or words below the blank.

1. His brother is _____ a
   (saying that it will happen)
   storm.

2. Those women _____ a
   (looked at)
   site for their new store.

3. They are trying to _____
   (get)
   oil from the sea.

4. A bird _____ its nest
   (builds)
   from twigs.

L EVIDENCE

Write the letter of the fact that explains why each thing happened.

> **A.** Jim told the action that things do.
> **B.** Fred named a thing.

1. He said a noun. _____

2. He said a word like **protection.** _____

3. He said a word like **select.** _____

4. He said a verb. _____

Lesson 23

A CONTRADICTIONS

Make each contradiction true.

Sam is taller than Bill.

1. Sam is shorter than Bill.
2. Sam is not taller than Bill.
3. Bill is taller than Sam.
4. Bill is not shorter than Sam.

B WRITING DIRECTIONS

Complete the instructions.

③ ②
ribs_____**skull**
①

1. Draw a _____ line.
2. Write the word _____ on the _____ end of the line.
3. Write the word _____ on the _____ end of the line.

C SENTENCE COMBINATIONS

Write **one** or **more than one** after each sentence. Write **hop** or **hops** in each blank.

1. Joan and Barry _____ over logs.

_____

2. She _____ over logs.

_____

3. His dad and her mom _____ over logs.

_____

4. This thin man _____ over logs.

_____

D DEDUCTIONS

Cross out the words that are in the rule and the conclusion. Then write the middle part.

1. Every person has a femur.

_____

So, Ted has a femur.

2. Every fish swims.

_____

So, a perch swims.

3. Every bone needs milk.

_____

So, a humerus needs milk.

E BODY SYSTEMS

Write **abdominal muscle, biceps,** or **quadriceps** in each blank.

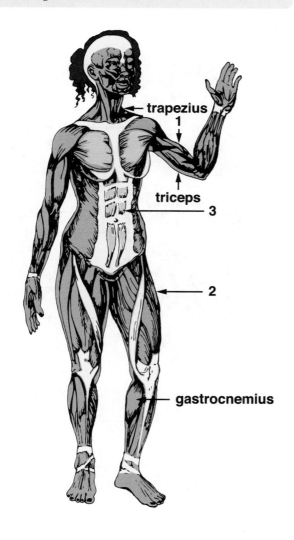

trapezius
1
triceps
3
2
gastrocnemius

1. _____

2. _____

3. _____

F PARTS OF SPEECH

Underline the nouns. Draw a line **over** the adjectives. Circle the verbs.

1. Her dad was constructing that home. (2)

2. Six banks will obtain some protection. (2)

3. A cop was mopping with a mop. (2)

4. An elephant was sitting in the forest. (2)

5. Elephants sat in forests. (2)

G DEFINITIONS

Write a word that comes from **construct** or **protect** in each blank. Then write **verb, noun,** or **adjective** after each item.

1. Those beavers are _____ a dam in the river.

   _____

2. A hat will _____ your ears from the cold.

   _____

3. Reading is a very

   _____ habit.

   _____

4. An artist made some plans for a big

   _____.

   _____

5. Mother hens have to

   _____ their chicks.

   _____

H **SENTENCE COMBINATIONS**

I **BODY SYSTEMS**

Underline the common part. Then combine the sentences with **and**.

Fill in each blank.

1. Andy chops logs for fun.
   Kim chops logs for fun.

   _____

   _____

2. An ape swings from trees.
   A monkey swings from trees.

   _____

   _____

3. Fred obtained stamps.
   Fred sent a letter.

   _____

   _____

4. That bee bites cows.
   This snake bites cows.

   _____

   _____

5. Lee picks corn.
   Lee pulls weeds.

   _____

   _____

6. Susan cleans yards for cash.
   Nancy cleans yards for cash.

   _____

   _____

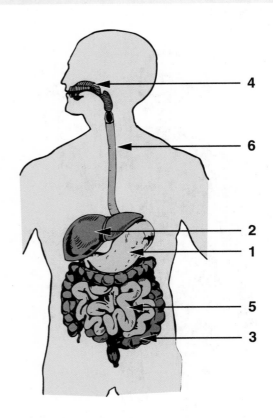

1. _____

2. _____

3. _____

4. _____

5. _____

6. _____

A WRITING DIRECTIONS

Complete the instructions.

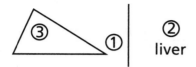
liver

1. Draw a _____ line.

2. Write the word _____

   to the _____ of the line.

3. Draw a _____ to the

   _____ of the line.

B BODY SYSTEMS

Write **gastrocnemius, trapezius,** or **triceps** in each blank.

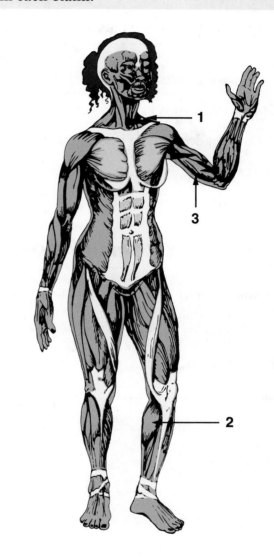

1. _____

2. _____

3. _____

C CONTRADICTIONS

Make each contradiction true.

> The quadriceps is in the muscular system.

1. The quadriceps is in the digestive system.
2. The quadriceps is in the system of bones.
3. A four-headed muscle is in the skeletal system.
4. The quadriceps is a bone.

D SENTENCE COMBINATIONS

Write **one** or **more than one** after each sentence. Write **sing** or **sings** in each blank.

1. His dad _____ well.

   _____

2. His dad and mom _____ well.

   _____

3. Those ten kids _____ well.

   _____

4. Her older brothers _____ well.

   _____

E DEDUCTIONS

Cross out the words that are in the rule and the conclusion. Then write the middle part.

1. Some <u>animals</u> have <u>bones</u>.

   _____

   So, maybe <u>clams</u> have <u>bones</u>.

2. Every <u>plant</u> is a <u>living thing</u>.

   _____

   So, a <u>fern</u> is a <u>living thing</u>.

3. Some <u>words</u> are <u>nouns</u>.

   _____

   So, maybe <u>gullet</u> is a <u>noun</u>.

F PARTS OF SPEECH

Underline the nouns. Draw a line **over** the adjectives. Circle the verbs.

1. The esophagus goes from the mouth to the stomach. (3)
2. Some nouns name things. (2)
3. A metal ship is rocking in the deep pond. (2)
4. Those shoppers selected some hats. (2)
5. That old shopper has a hat. (2)

G DEFINITIONS

Write a word that comes from **obtain** or **construct** in each blank. Then write **verb, noun,** or **adjective** after each item.

1. Lisa will _____ lots of cash when she sells her car.

   _____

2. The _____ of that home will take ten years.

   _____

3. Kim's mother gave her lots of

   _____ advice.

   _____

4. They are _____ some meat from the store.

   _____

5. A carpenter is _____ a bench with a hammer.

   _____

H ANALOGIES

Complete the analogies.

1. **Tell what body system each muscle is in.**

   Biceps are to _____

   as quadriceps are to _____

   _____.

2. **Tell how many heads each muscle has.**

   Biceps are to _____

   as quadriceps are to _____.

3. **Tell what bone each muscle covers.**

   Biceps are to _____

   as quadriceps are to _____.

I SENTENCE COMBINATIONS

Underline the common part. Then combine the sentences with **and**.

1. Tim loads boxes for the shop.
   Hector loads boxes for the shop.

   _____

   _____

2. This vet examines cracked femurs.
   That doctor examines cracked femurs.

   _____

   _____

   _____

3. Donna chopped logs.
   Donna started a fire.

   _____

   _____

4. Linda likes tall trees.
   Jane likes tall trees.

   _____

   _____

5. Locks protect homes from robbers.
   Gates protect homes from robbers.

   _____

   _____

   _____

6. Sam opened the door.
   Sam walked into the shop.

   _____

   _____

   _____

J FOLLOWING DIRECTIONS

Follow the directions.

1. In the box, draw a line that slants up to the left.

2. Draw a line that slants down to the left from the bottom of the first line.

3. Connect the slanted lines.

K INFERENCE

Read the story and answer the questions.
- Circle the **W** if the question is answered by words in the story. Then underline those words.
- Circle the **D** if the question is answered by a deduction.

If you don't get all the vitamins you need, you can get diseases. Children who don't get any vitamin D may get soft bones. This disease is called **rickets.**

Children with rickets have soft femurs. Sometimes their femurs get so soft that the femurs can't hold up the rest of their body. So the femurs start to bend. Instead of normal, straight femurs, children with rickets may have curved femurs. When the children stand up, their legs are bowed instead of straight.

---

1. What can happen if you don't get all the vitamins you need?

    _____

    _____ **W   D**

2. If Jim gets lots of vitamin D and Bill doesn't get any vitamin D, which person has stronger bones?

    _____ **W   D**

3. What may happen to your bones when you get rickets?

    _____

4. Is rickets bad for your femur?

    _____

5. What kind of bones do children with rickets have?

    _____

6. When people have rickets, what can't their leg bones do?

    _____

    _____

WORD LIST

abdominal muscle (n) a muscle that goes from the ribs to the pelvis
biceps (n) the muscle that covers the front of the humerus
constructive (a) that something is helpful
gastrocnemius (n) the muscle that covers the back of the lower leg
muscular system (n) the body system of muscles
quadriceps (n) the muscle that covers the front of the femur
predict (v) to say that something will happen
predictable (a) that something is easy to predict
prediction (n) a statement that predicts
reside (v) to live somewhere
trapezius (n) the muscle that covers the back of the neck
triceps (n) the muscle that covers the back of the humerus

A BODY RULES

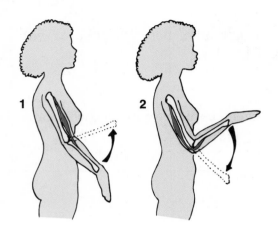

B WRITING DIRECTIONS

Complete the instructions.

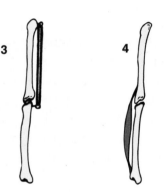

① _____

liver ③   ②

1. Draw a _____ line.

2. Draw a _____ below the
   _____ end of the line.

3. Write the word _____ below
   the _____ end of the line.

C SENTENCE COMBINATIONS

Write **one** or **more than one** after each
sentence. Write **talk** or **talks** in each blank.

1. She _____ fast.

   _____

2. That rabbit _____ fast.

   _____

3. That rabbit and this chipmunk

   _____ fast.

   _____

4. Six bosses _____ fast.

   _____

D DEDUCTIONS

Cross out the words that are in the rule and
the conclusion. Then write the middle part.

1. Insects do not have bones.

   _____

   So, ants do not have bones.

2. Some men have black hair.

   _____

   So, maybe Fred has black hair.

3. Every muscle pulls.

   _____

   So, the biceps pulls.

E DEFINITIONS

Write a word that comes from **reside** in each blank. Then write **verb, noun,** or **adjective** after each item.

1. Your home is your _____ .

   _____

2. Some birds _____ in nests.

   _____

3. You don't find lumber mills in

   _____ parts of town.

   _____

4. Some men work where they

   _____.

   _____

5. A shack is a cheap _____ .

   _____

F CONTRADICTIONS

Make each contradiction true.

> All dogs have a spine.

1. His dog does not have a backbone.

2. Only some dogs have a spine.

3. That puppy has no spine.

4. Just a few dogs have a spine.

G PARTS OF SPEECH

Underline the nouns. Draw a line **over** the adjectives. Circle the verbs.

1. The small intestine brings food to the blood. (3)

2. The intestines are in the digestive system. (2)

3. The digestive system is a body system. (2)

4. Those dogs were sitting. (1)

5. Those dogs were sitting on the porch. (2)

H ANALOGIES

Complete the analogy.

> **Build** is to **construct**

1. as **get** is to _____ ,

2. as **guard** is to _____ ,

3. as **look at** is to _____ .

I SENTENCE COMBINATIONS

Underline the common part. Then combine the sentences with **and.**

1. Joe got into bed.
   Joe went to sleep.

   _____

   _____

2. His dad plays tennis.
   Her mom plays tennis.

   _____

   _____

3. This dog slept.
   That cat slept.

   _____

   _____

4. Linda runs every day.
   Jean runs every day.

   _____

   _____

5. This goat smells bad.
   That sheep smells bad.

   _____

   _____

6. The man obtained six socks.
   The man obtained ten hats.

   _____

   _____

J FOLLOWING DIRECTIONS

Follow the directions.

1. Print a large **L** inside the box.

2. Draw a slanted line from the right end of the horizontal line to the top of the vertical line.

3. Write the word **triceps** inside the shape.

4. To the left of the vertical line, write the word **biceps.**

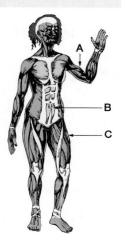

FACT GAME SCORECARD

1	2	3	4	5	6	7	8	9	10	11	12	13	14	15
16	17	18	19	20	21	22	23	24	25	26	27	28	29	30

FG   B   T

Fact Game 3

2. Answer the questions.

   a. What is the first part of a deduction called?

   b. What is the last part of a deduction called?

3. Complete the analogy by telling the adjective that comes from each verb.

   a. **Predict** is to ▮▮▮▮

   b. as **construct** is to ▮▮▮▮

   c. as **select** is to ▮▮▮▮

4. The sentence in the box is true. Which item contradicts the true sentence?

> Jacob hurt his trapezius.

   a. Jacob hurt a muscle in his neck.

   b. Jacob hurt a muscle in his leg.

5. Name the body systems.

   a. The system of muscles.

   b. The system of bones.

   c. The system that changes food into fuel.

6. Answer the questions.

   a. What verb means **to live somewhere?**

   b. What noun means **a statement that predicts?**

   c. What adjective means **that something is helpful?**

7. Combine the sentences with **and.**

Ahmed resides in a big city.
Narmeen resides in a big city.

8. Name the part of speech for each underlined word.

   a. The cat played with the <u>wool</u> sock.

   b. Francisco <u>predicted</u> that it would rain.

   c. My <u>friend</u> knocked on the door.

9. Complete each sentence with a word that comes from **predict.**

   a. The man on TV ▮▮▮▮ it would rain.

   b. That movie has a ▮▮▮▮ ending.

   c. They are ▮▮▮▮ that gas prices will go up.

10. Read the sentence and answer the questions.

> Ripe bananas have a yellow peel.

   a. What are the nouns?

   b. What are the adjectives?

   c. What is the verb?

11. Combine the sentences with **and.**

<u>The driver</u> slowed down.
<u>The driver</u> made a left turn.

12. Name the muscles A, B, and C in the picture.

Lesson 26

A WRITING DIRECTIONS

Complete the instructions.

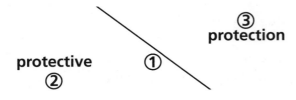

protection ③

protective ②

①

1. Draw a line that slants down to the

   _____ .

2. Write the word _____

   to the _____ of the line.

3. Write the word _____

   to the _____ of the line.

B PARTS OF SPEECH

Underline the nouns. Draw a line **over** the adjectives. Circle the verbs.

1. Some animals fly. (1)
2. Some animals are flying over trees. (2)
3. Six rabbits jumped over a bench. (2)
4. A small rabbit made a big jump. (2)
5. That rabbit is an animal. (2)

C BODY RULES

Circle each bone that will move. Then draw an arrow that shows which way the bone will move.

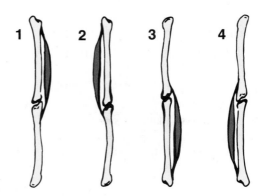

1 2 3 4

D CONTRADICTIONS

Underline each contradiction. Make each contradiction true.

Jim always selected books with predictable endings.

1. Jim always chose books with endings that were hard to predict.
2. Jim never selected books with endings that he could predict.
3. The books that Jim selected had endings that were easy to predict.
4. The books that Jim chose had endings that were never hard to predict.

94   *Lesson 26*

E SENTENCE COMBINATIONS

Write **who** or **which** after each item.

1. The construction _____
2. Her mom _____
3. Those dogs _____
4. His stomach _____
5. Her coat _____
6. An old man _____
7. A lemon _____
8. Three men _____
9. Three forks _____
10. Her hair _____

F DEDUCTIONS

Cross out the words that are in the rule and the conclusion, and then write the middle part.

1. Sid has every kind of tool.

   _____

   So, Sid has a hammer.

2. Barbara has some vehicles.

   _____

   So, maybe Barbara has a truck.

3. Some vehicles have pistons.

   _____

   So, maybe a boat has pistons.

G INFERENCE

Read the story and answer the questions.
- Circle the **W** if the question is answered by words in the story. Then underline those words.
- Circle the **D** if the question is answered by a deduction.

> The harder your body works, the more calories it needs. Carbohydrates, fats, and proteins give you calories. Vitamins and minerals don't give you calories. Most men need 2,500 calories a day. Most women need 2,000 calories a day.

1. When does your body need more calories?

_____

_____

2. If Bob runs a race and Ted sits at his desk, which person uses more calories?

_____ **W D**

3. How do you know?

_____

_____ **W D**

4. Which nutrients give you calories?

_____

_____ **W D**

5. Who needs more calories a day, most men or most women?

_____

6. How many more?

_____ **W D**

H DEFINITIONS

Write a word that comes from **predict** in each blank. Then write **verb, noun,** or **adjective** after each item.

1. The reporter made _____ about the weather.

_____

2. An old man is _____ a rotten summer for fishing.

_____

3. The ending of the story was not

_____.

_____

4. Bill is _____ that the old bus will fall apart.

_____

5. Pat hopes her _____ about the game will come true.

_____

I ANALOGIES

Complete the analogy.

Biceps is to two

1. as triceps is to _____ ,

2. as quadriceps is to _____ .

J EVIDENCE

Write the letter of the fact that explains why each thing happened.

A. Ron is building up his quadriceps.
B. Joe broke his humerus.

1. He runs every day. _____

2. He has a cast on his arm. _____

3. He was in the hospital for a week. _____

4. He can't lift barbells. _____

K BODY SYSTEMS

Fill in each blank.

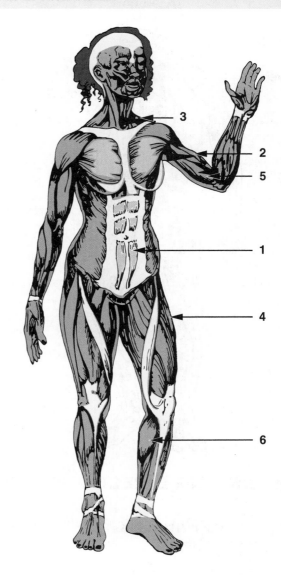

1. _____

2. _____

3. _____

4. _____

5. _____

6. _____

A BODY SYSTEMS

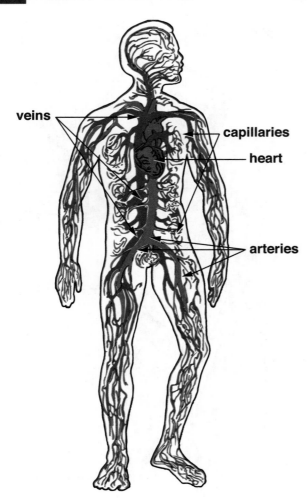

veins
capillaries
heart
arteries

B WRITING DIRECTIONS

Complete the instructions.

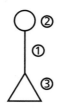

① ② ③

1. Draw a _____ line.

2. Draw a circle _____ the line.

3. Draw a triangle _____ the line.

C EVIDENCE

Write **R** for each fact that is **relevant** to what happened. Write **I** for each fact that is **irrelevant** to what happened.

> The dog bit the sailor.

1. The sailor was mean to the dog before the dog bit her. _____

2. The dog had brown spots. _____

3. The sailor was forty-two years old. _____

4. The dog didn't like people. _____

D DEFINITIONS

Write a word that comes from **select** or **predict** in each blank. Then write **verb, noun,** or **adjective** after each item.

1. The big city had a wide _____

   of concerts._____

2. The movie was so _____ that everyone figured out the ending.

   _____

3. If you want to _____ a new shirt, you have to go to the store.

   _____

4. His dad _____ that it would rain.

   _____

5. His dad's _____ made Jim feel sad. _____

E SENTENCE COMBINATIONS

Write **one** or **more than one** after each sentence. Write **were** or **was** in each blank.

1. Ned _____ running.

   _____

2. Ned and Jane _____ running.

   _____

3. A deer _____ running.

   _____

4. Ten cars _____ running.

   _____

F CONTRADICTIONS

Underline each contradiction. Make each contradiction true.

> That dog never protects this shed.

1. The dog always gives this shed protection.

2. This shed is never protected by that dog.

3. That dog sometimes protects this shed.

4. This shed is always guarded by that dog.

G SENTENCE COMBINATIONS

Write **who** or **which** after each item.

1. Her femur _____

2. Her baby _____

3. That man _____

4. His desk _____

5. Their residence _____

6. A grape _____

7. My liver _____

8. Five trees _____

9. Some glue _____

10. His big sister _____

H DEDUCTIONS

Cross out the words that are in the rule and the conclusion. Then write the middle part.

1. Some adjectives tell what kind.

   _____

   So, maybe **rotund** tells what kind.

2. Every verb tells the action that things do.

   _____

   So, **protect** tells the action that things do.

3. The man had some bones.

   _____

   So, maybe the man had a femur.

I PARTS OF SPEECH

Underline the nouns. Draw a line **over** the adjectives. Circle the verbs.

1. Kids looked at that construction. (2)

2. Carpenters constructed that home. (2)

3. Those women are constructing homes. (2)

4. His pal constructs boxes. (2)

5. Her pals play in that construction. (2)

J DEDUCTIONS

Use the rule to answer the questions.

> The more you work a muscle, the stronger it gets.

1. Bob's muscles are weaker than Steve's.
   a. Which person works his muscles more?

   _____

   b. How do you know?

   _____

   _____

   _____

2. Cathy works her quadriceps 10 minutes a day. Sue works her quadriceps 25 minutes a day.
   a. Which person has stronger quadriceps?

   _____

   b. How do you know?

   _____

   _____

   _____

3. Bill can lift big boxes. Jack can lift only small boxes.
   a. Which person works his muscles more?

   _____

   b. How do you know?

   _____

   _____

K BODY RULES

Circle each bone that will move. Then draw an arrow that shows which way the bone will move.

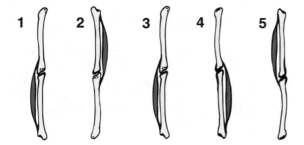

L BODY SYSTEMS

Fill in each blank.

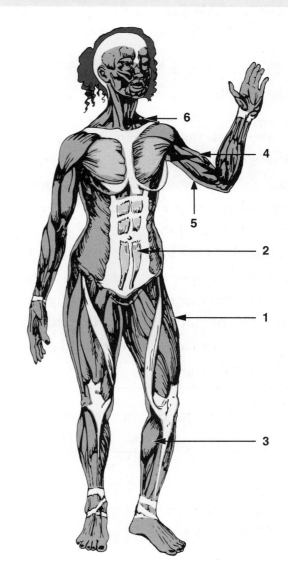

1. _____

2. _____

3. _____

4. _____

5. _____

6. _____

M **INFERENCE**

Read the story and answer the questions.
- Circle the **W** if the question is answered by words in the story. Then underline those words.
- Circle the **D** if the question is answered by a deduction.

You know that your circulatory system moves blood to all parts of your body. It takes blood to your brain, to your toes, to your triceps, to your stomach. All these parts need blood to work.

The blood has many things in it. One of the most important things is the food you eat. Your digestive system brings food to the blood. It changes the food so that the blood can carry the food to all parts of the body.

---

1. What does your circulatory system do?

_____

_____ **W   D**

2. Name at least six body parts that need blood to work.

_____

_____

_____

3. What is one of the most important things your blood has?

_____

_____ **W   D**

4. What does your digestive system do?

_____

_____

5. Why does your digestive system change food?

_____

_____

_____ **W   D**

6. Does the circulatory system change food?

_____

7. Do your triceps need food to work?

_____ **W   D**

D EVIDENCE

Write **R** for each fact that is **relevant** to what happened. Write **I** for each fact that is **irrelevant** to what happened.

> The woman honked her horn.

1. She had a red car. _____
2. She was mad at the driver in front of her. _____
3. She was wearing a silk hat. _____
4. She liked to make noise. _____

E SENTENCE COMBINATIONS

Write **one** or **more than one** after each sentence. Write **were** or **was** in each blank.

1. A fat cat _____ eating.

   _____

2. His cats _____ eating.

   _____

3. His cats and dogs _____ eating.

   _____

4. My dog _____ eating.

   _____

F SENTENCE COMBINATIONS

Underline the common part. Then combine the sentences with **and.**

1. The man was sad.
   His wife was sad.

   _____

   _____

2. Roy was running.
   Fred was running.

   _____

   _____

3. Frogs were hopping on pads.
   Toads were hopping on pads.

   _____

   _____

4. Her dad went to the store.
   Her dad obtained five shirts.

   _____

   _____

5. Irma swims in that pond.
   Linda swims in that pond.

   _____

   _____

6. Pat was sleeping in class.
   Jack was sleeping in class.

   _____

   _____

G ANALOGIES

Complete the analogies.

1. **Tell what part of speech each word is.**

   Protection is to _____,

   as **selection** is to _____.

2. **Tell the verb that each word comes from.**

   Protection is to _____,

   as **selection** is to _____.

3. **Tell how many letters each word has.**

   Protection is to _____,

   as **selection** is to _____.

H BODY RULES

Circle each bone that will move. Then draw an arrow that shows which way the bone will move.

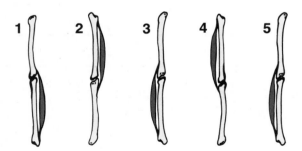

I BODY SYSTEMS

Fill in each blank.

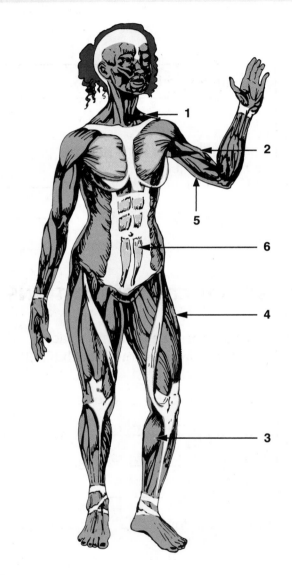

1. _____

2. _____

3. _____

4. _____

5. _____

6. _____

J DEFINITIONS

Write a word that comes from **criticize** or **construct** in each blank. Then write **verb, noun,** or **adjective** after each item.

1. Linda's brother likes to _____ her work.

    _____

2. Her brother's many _____ hurt Linda's feelings.

    _____

3. So Linda is _____ a bunch of earplugs.

    _____

4. Linda thinks that her earplugs are some of

    the most _____
    tools ever made.

    _____

5. Now she never has to hear her brother's

    _____ remarks.

    _____

K DEDUCTIONS

Cross out the words that are in the rule and the conclusion. Then write the middle part.

1. Some <u>plants</u> can grow without <u>sun</u>.

    _____

    So, maybe a <u>fern</u> can grow without <u>sun</u>.

2. <u>Bill</u> examined some <u>muscles</u>.

    _____

    So, maybe <u>Bill</u> examined a <u>trapezius</u>.

3. <u>Nouns</u> do not tell <u>how many</u>.

    _____

    So, **protection** does not tell <u>how many</u>.

L **INFERENCE**

Read the story and answer the questions.
- Circle the **W** if the question is answered by words in the story. Then underline those words.
- Circle the **D** if the question is answered by a deduction.

Your digestive system changes food so that the blood can carry the food to all parts of the body. Solid food, like hamburgers and carrots, has to be made liquid (like milk or soda pop) before the blood can carry it. The first way you make solid food liquid is by cutting it with your teeth. Your teeth are like sharp blades, and they cut the food into small bits. The smaller the bit, the easier it is to make it liquid.

---

1. Why does the digestive system change food?

_____

_____

_____ **W** **D**

2. Name five solid foods.

_____

_____

_____

3. Name five liquid foods.

_____

_____

_____

4. What does the digestive system do to solid food?

_____

5. What do your teeth do to the food?

_____

_____ **W** **D**

6. Which is easier to make liquid, a big chunk of ham or a small chunk of ham?

_____ **W** **D**

A WRITING DIRECTIONS

Complete the instructions.

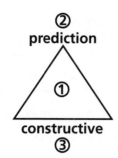

② prediction

①

constructive ③

1. Draw a _____.

2. Write the word **prediction** _____

   the _____.

3. Write the word **constructive** _____

   the _____.

B PARTS OF SPEECH

Underline the nouns. Draw **one** line over the adjectives. Draw **two** lines over the articles. Circle the verbs.

1. The old woman made a large fireplace.

2. Some red roses are growing in the yard.

3. An excellent singer sang the fast tune.

4. A banana rotted in the big bowl.

5. Angry bees buzzed around her head.

C BODY RULES

Draw in the muscles.

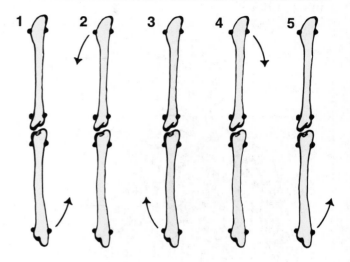

1 2 3 4 5

D BODY SYSTEMS

Write **arteries, veins, heart,** or **capillaries** in each blank.

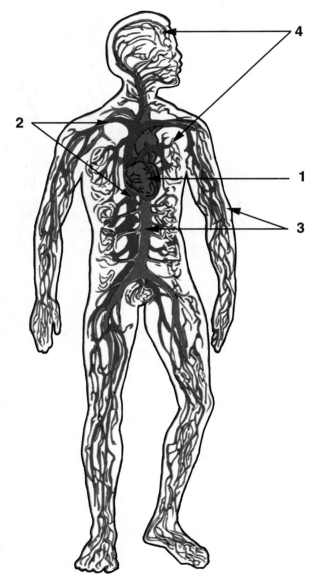

1. _____

2. _____

3. _____

4. _____

E EVIDENCE

Write **R** for each fact that is **relevant** to what happened. Write **I** for each fact that is **irrelevant** to what happened.

> The cook burned the potatoes.

1. He didn't put any butter in the pan. _____

2. He liked big dinners. _____

3. He put the burner on high. _____

4. He was wearing a big white hat. _____

5. He had never cooked potatoes before. _____

F CONTRADICTIONS

Make each statement mean the same thing as the statement in the box.

> The selective shopper obtained a better car.

1. The careless shopper got a better car.

2. The shopper who was careful got a better car.

3. The careful shopper got a car that was worse.

4. The shopper who obtained a better car was selective.

G SENTENCE COMBINATIONS

Underline the common part. Then combine the sentences with **who** or **which.**

1. She hurt her trapezius.
   Her trapezius covers the back of her neck.

   _____

   _____

   _____

   _____

2. He criticized Linda.
   Linda was standing on his toe.

   _____

   _____

   _____

3. Tom is very protective of his little brother.
   His little brother is only six weeks old.

   _____

   _____

   _____

   _____

4. The old woman obtained those roses.
   Those roses were yellow.

   _____

   _____

   _____

5. Tom's mother is calling for Tom. Tom is under the bed.

   _____

   _____

   _____

H INFERENCE

Read the story and answer the questions.
- Circle the **W** if the question is answered by words in the story. Then underline those words.
- Circle the **D** if the question is answered by a deduction.

After the teeth cut the food into small bits, the bits go down the esophagus and into the stomach. You can understand how the stomach works if you think of what happens when you put a bit of black dirt into a glass of clear water. The dirt gets softer and softer. If you stir the dirt, the water will turn black. The stomach does the same thing to food. It mixes the food with different chemicals that make the food soft. Then it stirs everything up.

1. What happens to dirt when you put it in water?

_____

_____ **W** **D**

2. What happens to the water when you stir the dirt?

_____ **W** **D**

3. Where does the food go after it is cut into small bits?

_____

_____ **W** **D**

4. What happens to food when it gets into the stomach?

_____

5. If the liquids in your stomach are clear and the food that comes in is black, what color will the liquid turn?

_____

6. If the liquids in your stomach are clear and they turn green after the food comes in, what color is the food?

_____

I SENTENCE COMBINATIONS

Underline the common part. Then combine the sentences with **and**.

1. Melba was thinking hard.
   Liz was thinking hard.

   _____

   _____

2. The zoo was closed.
   The zoo was locked.

   _____

   _____

3. That man takes a walk each day.
   His dog takes a walk each day.

   _____

   _____

4. The coach was on the track.
   Her players were on the track.

   _____

   _____

   _____

5. Ted was cheering.
   Linda was cheering.

   _____

   _____

6. An old goat ate ten apples.
   An old goat ate six pears.

   _____

   _____

J DEDUCTIONS

Write the conclusion of each deduction.

1. Some muscles cover a bone. The abdominal muscle is a muscle.

   So, _____

   _____

   _____.

2. Everything you eat goes down your esophagus. Salad is a thing you eat.

   So, _____

   _____.

3. Fred has some plants. Mums are plants.

   So, _____

   _____.

K FOLLOWING DIRECTIONS

Follow the directions.

```
┌─────────────────────────────┐
│                             │
│                             │
│                             │
│                             │
└─────────────────────────────┘
```

1. Draw a vertical line in the box.

2. Draw a horizontal line to the left of the vertical line.

3. Write the word **circulatory** above the right end of the horizontal line.

L DEFINITIONS

Fill in each blank with the word that has the same meaning as the word or words under the blank.

1. Some _____ can be helpful.
   (statements that criticize)

2. For fifty dollars Helen can _____
   a dress.   (get)

3. If you are careful when you _____
   a car, you will save cash.   (choose)

4. Some mice _____ in walls.
                    (live)

M CONTRADICTIONS

Underline each contradiction. Make each contradiction true.

> The biceps covers only the front of the humerus.

1. A two-headed muscle covers the front of the leg bone.

2. The biceps does not cover the back of the humerus.

3. Part of the lower arm bone is covered by the biceps.

4. A four-headed muscle covers the front of the humerus.

WORD LIST

arteries (n) the tubes that carry blood away from the heart

capillaries (n) the very small tubes that connect the arteries and veins

circulatory system (n) the system that moves blood around the body

critical (a) that something criticizes

criticism (n) a statement that criticizes

criticize (v) to find fault with

heart (n) the pump that moves the blood

predict (v) to say that something will happen

reside (v) to live somewhere

residence (n) a place where someone resides

residential (a) that a place has many residences

veins (n) the tubes that carry blood back to the heart

D CONTRADICTIONS

Make each statement mean the same thing as the statement in the box.

> Bob wants to build up his quadriceps.

1. Bob wants to build up his arm muscles.

2. Bob wants to make his leg muscles bigger.

3. Bob wants to build up the muscles that cover his humerus.

4. Bob wants to make his leg muscles weaker.

E DEFINITIONS

Write a word that comes from **criticize** in each blank. Then write **verb, noun,** or **adjective** after each item.

1. The reviewer was paid to _____ the movie.

   _____

2. The reviewer's only _____ was that the movie was too short.

   _____

3. He did not like to write _____ reviews.

   _____

4. Now the reviewer's boss is

   _____ his review.

   _____

5. "This review is not _____ enough," the boss said.

   _____

F SENTENCE COMBINATIONS

Write **one** or **more than one** after each sentence. Write **is** or **are** in each blank.

1. Those women _____ tall.

   _____

2. This pole _____ tall.

   _____

3. This pole and that fence _____ tall.

   _____

4. His brothers _____ tall.

   _____

G BODY RULES

Draw in the muscles.

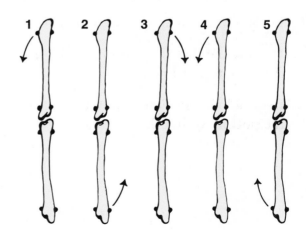

H EVIDENCE

Write **R** for each fact that is **relevant** to what happened. Write **I** for each fact that is **irrelevant** to what happened.

There were mice in the kitchen.

1. The walls were painted white. _____

2. There was a hole in the wall. _____

3. The food was left uncovered. _____

4. There weren't any traps. _____

5. The kitchen was very big. _____

I FOLLOWING DIRECTIONS

Follow the directions.

1. Draw a line that slants up to the left.

2. Draw a line that slants down to the left from the top of line **1.**

3. Draw a line that slants up to the left from the bottom of line **2.**

J DEDUCTIONS

Use the rule to answer the questions.

The more meat you eat, the more protein you get.

1. John ate two quarter-pound hamburgers. Melba ate one quarter-pound hamburger.
   a. Who got more protein from meat?

   _____

   b. How do you know?

   _____

   _____

2. Sue gets thirty grams of protein a day from meat. Carol gets seventy grams of protein a day from meat.
   a. Who eats more meat?

   _____

   b. How do you know?

   _____

   _____

3. Andy eats three pounds of meat a week. Eric eats five pounds of meat a week.
   a. Who gets more protein from meat?

   _____

   b. How do you know?

   _____

   _____

K INFERENCE

Read the story and answer the questions.
- Circle the **W** if the question is answered by words in the story. Then underline those words.
- Circle the **D** if the question is answered by a deduction.

After the stomach has made the food liquid, the food goes into the small intestine. The walls of the small intestine are lined with capillaries. As the food goes down the small intestine, the capillaries soak up the parts of the food that the blood needs. The food that the capillaries don't soak up goes on to the large intestine, where the food is turned into solid waste.

1. When does the food go into the small intestine?

   _____

   _____

   _____ **W   D**

2. What are the walls of the small intestine covered with?

   _____ **W   D**

3. How do the capillaries get the parts of the food that the blood needs?

   _____

4. Where does the rest of the food go?

   _____

   _____ **W   D**

5. What does the large intestine do to food?

   _____

   _____

6. Which system brings food to the blood?

   _____

7. Which system carries blood to all parts of the body?

   _____

L **BODY SYSTEMS**

Write **arteries, heart, veins,** or **capillaries** in each blank.

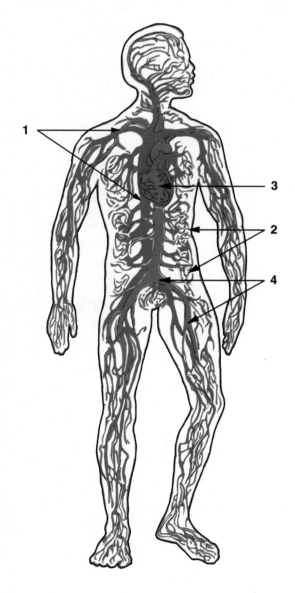

1. _____

2. _____

3. _____

4. _____

A BODY SYSTEMS

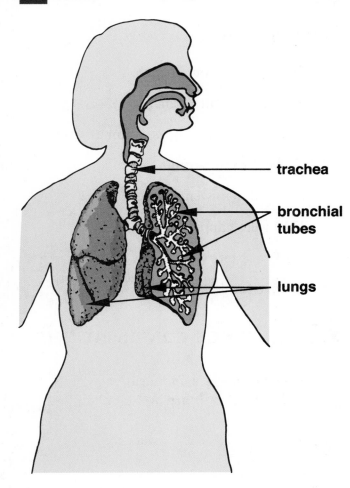

trachea

bronchial tubes

lungs

C ANALOGIES

Write what each analogy tells.

- what part of speech each word is
- what verb each word comes from
- what ending each word has

1. **Protection** is to **ion** as **residence** is to **ence.**

_____

_____

2. **Protection** is to noun as **residence** is to noun.

_____

_____

3. **Protection** is to **protect** as **residence** is to **reside.**

_____

_____

B CONTRADICTIONS

Tell which fact each statement contradicts.

A. Some birds cannot fly.
B. All birds have only two legs.

1. That bird ran on four legs. _____

2. All birds fly at night. _____

3. Every bird flies. _____

4. His bird stood on three legs. _____

D BODY RULES

Draw in the muscles.

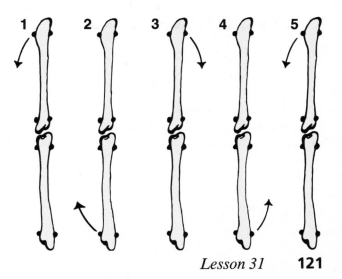

E FOLLOWING DIRECTIONS

Follow the directions.

> The tall girl ate cake.

1. Circle the words that tell what kind of girl ate cake.

2. Draw a line under the words that tell who ate cake.

3. Draw a line over the words that tell what the tall girl did.

4. Cross out the word that tells what the girl ate.

F DEDUCTIONS

Write the middle part of each deduction.

1. Some veins carry dark blood.

   _____

   So, maybe the vena cava carries dark blood.

2. Some animals have a circulatory system.

   _____

   So, maybe insects have a circulatory system.

3. The doctor looked at some arteries.

   _____

   So, maybe the doctor looked at an aorta.

G SUBJECT/PREDICATE

Circle the subject.

1. Three girls sat on a bench.

2. Five girls sat on a bench.

3. Five girls and two boys sat on a bench.

4. He went to the store.

5. That old man went to the store.

6. They were happy.

7. His five sisters were happy.

8. His five brothers sing well.

H SENTENCE COMBINATIONS

Write **one** or **more than one** after each sentence. Write **is** or **are** in each blank.

1. A goat _____ walking.

   _____

2. Bill and Linda _____ walking.

   _____

3. Her pal _____ walking.

   _____

4. Men _____ walking.

   _____

I SENTENCE COMBINATIONS

Underline the common part. Then combine the sentences with **who** or **which.**

1. The doctor examined Bill's veins.
   Bill's veins looked darker than normal.

   _____

   _____

   _____

2. Five tall girls play ball in that park.
   That park has a large field.

   _____

   _____

   _____

3. Tom selected some roses for George.
   George is sick.

   _____

   _____

   _____

4. Jill protects her bike.
   Her bike is worth a lot.

   _____

   _____

   _____

5. Ten boys constructed that shed.
   That shed is hidden by trees.

   _____

   _____

   _____

J CONTRADICTIONS

Make each contradiction true.

Sam hurt only the muscle in his upper leg.

1. Sam hurt his trapezius.

2. Sam hurt an arm muscle.

3. Sam's quadriceps was hurt.

4. Sam hurt his upper leg.

K SENTENCE COMBINATIONS

Underline the common part. Then combine the sentences with **and.**

1. Jan has big feet.
   Don has big feet.

   _____

   _____

2. Bill has black hair.
   Linda has black hair.

   _____

   _____

3. His mother has a new dress.
   His mother has an old ring.

   _____

   _____

4. Mike is constructing a shed.
   Ann is constructing a shed.

   _____

   _____

5. This woman was selecting hats.
   That man was selecting hats.

   _____

   _____

6. An elephant has big ears.
   A bat has big ears.

   _____

   _____

L BODY SYSTEMS

Fill in each blank.

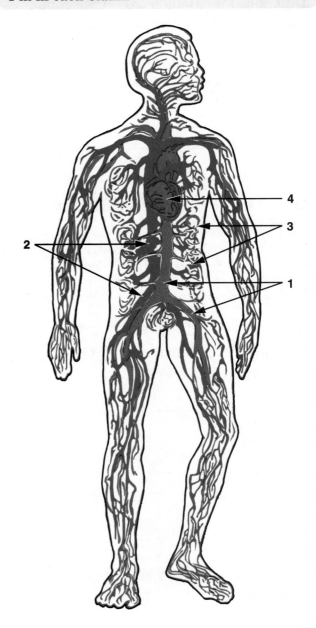

1. _____

2. _____

3. _____

4. _____

M EVIDENCE

Write **R** for each fact that is **relevant** to what happened. Write **I** for each fact that is **irrelevant** to what happened.

| The man walked with a limp. |

1. He had pulled his trapezius playing football. _____

2. He had a red shirt. _____

3. He had pulled his quadriceps playing basketball. _____

4. His boots were squeezing his feet. _____

5. He had a pain in his liver. _____

N DEFINITIONS

Write a word that comes from **produce** in each blank. Then write **verb, noun,** or **adjective** after each item.

1. Joe is _____ a film. .

   _____

2. Sue and Ann are a very _____

   team. _____

3. Sometimes farmers _____

   more grain than we need. _____

4. The _____ of cars is a big

   industry. _____

5. He was selective about what he

   _____ . _____

o **INFERENCE**

Read the story and answer the questions.
- Circle the **W** if the question is answered by words in the story. Then underline those words.
- Circle the **D** if the question is answered by a deduction.

You know there are 13 kinds of vitamins: A, C, D, E, K, and 8 kinds of B vitamins.

Here's a rule about vitamin A: If you don't get the right amount of vitamin A, you can't see well in the dark. You can also get bad eye diseases. Vitamin A comes from eggs, milk, carrots, spinach, and other foods. You may not like carrots and spinach, but they are good for you. Eating carrots and spinach is better than not seeing well.

---

1. What are the 13 kinds of vitamins?

_____

_____ **W** **D**

2. What two things can happen if you don't get enough vitamin A?

_____

_____

_____

_____

3. Rasheed ate eggs, and Ron ate a piece of ham. Which person got more vitamin A?

_____ **W** **D**

4. Pam can't see well in the dark. List four foods she needs to eat.

_____

_____

5. Which is better, eating spinach or not seeing well?

_____

E SENTENCE COMBINATIONS

Underline the common part. Circle the
word that combines the sentences correctly.
Combine the sentences with that word.

1. Jean constructed a bird feeder.
    Jean constructed that stool.
    and　　　**who**　　　**which**

    _____

    _____

    _____

2. The doctor examined Michiko's femur.
    Michiko's femur was broken.
    and　　　**who**　　　**which**

    _____

    _____

    _____

3. The coach was tired.
    The players were tired.
    and　　　**who**　　　**which**

    _____

    _____

    _____

4. That CD was scratched.
    John obtained that CD.
    and　　　**who**　　　**which**

    _____

    _____

F ANALOGIES

Write what each analogy tells.

> • what body system each part is in
> • how many of each part you have
> • what bone each part covers

1. Triceps are to two as quadriceps are
    to two.

    _____

    _____

2. Triceps are to humerus as quadriceps are
    to femur.

    _____

    _____

3. Triceps are to muscular system as
    quadriceps are to muscular system.

    _____

    _____

G DEDUCTIONS

Write the middle part of each deduction.

1. Most arteries carry fresh blood.

    _____

    So, maybe the hepatics carry fresh blood.

2. Fred did not look at any muscles.

    _____

    So, Fred did not look at a triceps.

3. Alice has every kind of vein.

    _____

    So, Alice has a vena cava.

　　　　Lesson 32　　**129**

H INFERENCE

Read the story and answer the questions.
- Circle the **W** if the question is answered by words in the story. Then underline those words.
- Circle the **D** if the question is answered by a deduction.

> You know that if you don't get any vitamin C you can get a disease called scurvy. When you have scurvy, skin cuts heal poorly, your gums bleed, and you get very weak. A long time ago, sailors got **scurvy** because they did not eat any fresh foods with vitamin C, such as lemons and limes. In 1795, the British king ordered all British sailors to start eating fresh lemons and limes. The sailors who ate lemons and limes didn't get scurvy.

1. What disease can you get if you don't get vitamin C?

   _____ **W D**

2. If skin cuts heal poorly and your gums bleed, what vitamin aren't you getting?

   _____

3. If Fred gets lots of vitamin C and Bill gets no vitamin C, which person will get scurvy?

   _____ **W D**

4. Why did sailors get scurvy a long time ago?

   _____

   _____

   _____ **W D**

5. Which king ordered sailors to start eating lemons?

   _____

6. About how many years ago did this happen?

   200   100   2000   50   **W D**

I BODY RULES

Draw in the muscles.

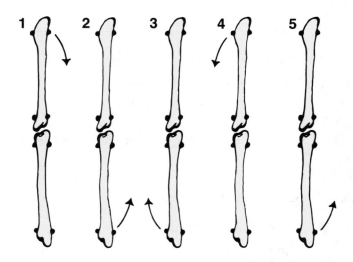

J DEFINITIONS

Write a word that comes from **reside** or **protect** in each blank. Then write **verb, noun,** or **adjective** after each item.

1. Six men are _____ in that
   cabin. _____

2. They have obtained a big dog to
   _____ the cabin.
   _____

3. But the dog is so lazy that it doesn't give
   the cabin any _____ at all.
   _____

4. In fact, the men's _____
   was robbed six times in three days.
   _____

5. The men think that they will get
   better _____ if they get a
   cat. _____

K BODY SYSTEMS

Fill in each blank.

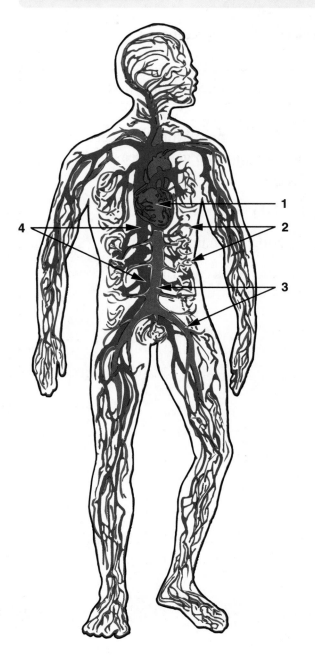

1. _____
2. _____
3. _____
4. _____

L EVIDENCE

Write **R** for each fact that is **relevant** to what happened. Write **I** for each fact that is **irrelevant** to what happened.

> The driver jammed on his brakes.

1. He was driving a blue car. _____

2. A dog had run in front of his car. _____

3. He didn't want to hit the dog. _____

4. The dog was named Bobo. _____

5. The driver was wearing a black coat. _____

A CONTRADICTIONS

Tell which fact each statement contradicts. Make each contradiction true.

> A. Only your biceps bends your arm.
> B. The biceps covers only the front of the humerus.

1. A two-headed muscle covers the front of the upper leg bone. _____

2. Part of the lower arm bone is covered by the biceps. _____

3. A three-headed muscle bends your arm. _____

4. The front of the humerus is not covered by a muscle. _____

B SENTENCE COMBINATIONS

Underline the common part. Circle the sentence that tells **why.** Combine the sentences with **because.**

1. Tom ate ten cans of beans.
Tom was hungry.

_____

_____

_____

2. Ron slipped.
Ron hurt his gastrocnemius.

_____

_____

_____

3. Their blood does not move well.
Their arteries are clogged.

_____

_____

_____

4. Mrs. Smith is looking for a big residence.
Mrs. Smith has ten kids.

_____

_____

_____

C BODY SYSTEMS

Write **trachea, lungs,** or **bronchial tubes** in each blank.

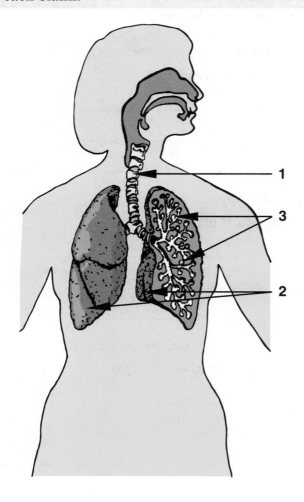

1. _____

2. _____

3. _____

D PARTS OF SPEECH

Underline the nouns. Draw **one** line **over** the adjectives. Draw **two** lines **over** the articles. Circle the verbs.

1. Cats like his dog.

2. The muscular system includes the abdominal muscle.

3. A broken femur needs a cast.

4. An older person has more time and wisdom.

5. The small intestine brings food to the blood.

E FOLLOWING DIRECTIONS

Follow the directions.

> The man chose a constructive book.

1. Cross out the words that tell what kind of book.

2. Underline the word that means **selected.**

3. Above the second crossed-out word, write a word that means the same thing.

4. Draw a line over the first article in the sentence.

F DEDUCTIONS

Write the middle part of each deduction.

1. A muscle does not move the bone it covers.

   _____

   So, the triceps does not move the bone it covers.

2. Most people have hair.

   _____

   So, maybe Bob has hair.

3. Tracy had some animals.

   _____

   So, maybe Tracy had a snake.

G SENTENCE COMBINATIONS

Underline the common part. Circle the word that combines the sentences correctly. Combine the sentences with that word.

1. The wall protected the city.
   The city had many battles.
   and   who   which

   _____

   _____

   _____

2. Len has ten books.
   Len has five pens.
   and   who   which

   _____

   _____

3. Tony has black hair.
   Jane has black hair.
   and   who   which

   _____

   _____

4. That woman resides in a tent.
   Her cat resides in a tent.
   and   who   which

   _____

   _____

5. Mary was not feeling well.
   Ted talked to Mary.
   and   who   which

   _____

   _____

   _____

H SENTENCE COMBINATIONS

Write **one** or **more than one** after each sentence. Write **have** or **has** in each blank.

1. They _____ some gold.

   _____

2. Mrs. Smith and Mr. Jones _____ some gold. _____

3. Six miners _____ some gold.

   _____

4. Mike _____ some gold.

   _____

I BODY RULES

Draw in the muscles.

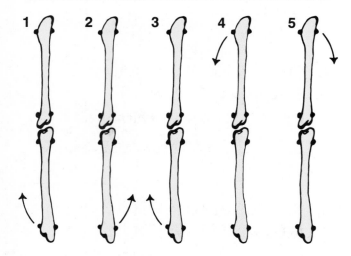

J CONTRADICTIONS

Make each statement mean the same thing as the statement in the box.

> People paid Linda to protect their residences.

1. Linda was paid to protect people's homes.

2. People paid Linda to guard the places where they worked.

3. Linda paid people to protect their places of residence.

4. People gave money to Linda for protecting their residences.

K ANALOGIES

Write what each analogy tells.

- what part of speech each word is
- what ending each word has
- what verb each word comes from

1. **Prediction** is to **ion** as **constructive** is to **ive.**

_____

_____

2. **Prediction** is to **noun** as **constructive** is to **adjective.**

_____

_____

3. **Prediction** is to **predict** as **constructive** is to **construct.**

_____

_____

L DEFINITIONS

Fill in each blank with the word that has the same meaning as the word or words under the blank.

1. If you know where the muscle is, you can

_____ which way the
   (say that it will happen)
bone will move.

2. Donna's mother _____
                    (found fault with)
her for making a mess.

3. Ribs _____ the organs
          (guard)
inside the chest.

4. He _____ in an old
        (lives)
building.

M EVIDENCE

Write **R** for each fact that is **relevant** to what happened. Write **I** for each fact that is **irrelevant** to what happened.

Bob woke up at 6 A.M.

1. He had to get up early. _____

2. He was six feet tall. _____

3. He had to be at work by 7 a.m. _____

4. His boss wanted everyone to
be on time. _____

N SUBJECT/PREDICATE

Circle the subject.

1. Six old men were playing ball.

2. Old men play ball.

3. He was happy.

4. He was always on time for class.

5. His tall sister was never late for class.

6. They made six kites.

7. Bill, Velma, and Liz have to obtain some food.

8. Your body needs sleep.

ⓞ INFERENCE

Read the story and answer the questions.
- Circle the **W** if the question is answered by words in the story. Then underline those words.
- Circle the **D** if the question is answered by a deduction.

> When you cut yourself, you stop bleeding because your blood clots. When your blood clots, it becomes thick and sticky. It makes a little dam that stops the blood from going out of the cut. People whose blood does not clot bleed a lot every time they get a cut. Here's a rule about vitamin K and blood: If you don't get any vitamin K, your blood won't clot. Vitamin K comes from eggs, spinach, and liver.

1. When does your blood clot?

_____

_____ **W   D**

2. What does your blood make when it clots?

_____ **W   D**

3. If somebody bleeds and bleeds every time he cuts himself, what isn't his blood doing?

_____

4. What vitamin helps your blood to clot?

_____

5. If Barbara doesn't get any vitamin K, what will happen to her blood when she cuts herself?

_____

6. What foods can Barbara eat to help her blood clot?

_____

_____ **W   D**

D SENTENCE COMBINATIONS

Underline the common part. Circle the sentence that tells **why.** Combine the sentences with **because.**

1. The man yelled.
The man hurt himself.

_____

_____

_____

2. Tim wants to construct a shack.
Tim obtained some tools.

_____

_____

_____

3. Terry is too critical.
Terry has no pals.

_____

_____

_____

4. Eve was thirsty.
Eve drank lots of water.

_____

_____

_____

E BODY RULES

Circle each bone that will move. Then draw an arrow that shows which way the bone will move.

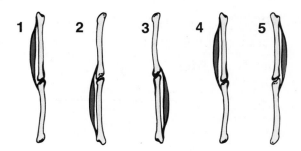

F FOLLOWING DIRECTIONS

Follow the directions.

This muscle covers the femur.

1. Cross out the words that tell what covers the femur.

2. Above the crossed-out words, write the name of the muscle that covers the femur.

3. Underline the word that means the upper leg bone.

4. Circle the verb.

G SENTENCE COMBINATIONS

Underline the common part. Circle the word that combines the sentences correctly. Combine the sentences with that word.

1. This man wants to reside in town.
That woman wants to reside in town.
and   who   which

_____

_____

_____

2. The digestive system changes food into fuel.
The liver is part of the digestive system.
and   who   which

_____

_____

_____

3. Fred is eating corn.
Bill is eating corn.
and   who   which

_____

_____

4. His mom was tired.
Her dad was tired.
and   who   which

_____

_____

5. Jim talked to that man.
That man was a sailor.
and   who   which

_____

_____

H EVIDENCE

Write **R** for each fact that is **relevant** to what happened. Write **I** for each fact that is **irrelevant** to what happened.

Bill's car didn't start.

1. His car had red carpeting.   _____

2. There was a hole in his gas tank.   _____

3. Some of the spark plug wires were broken.   _____

4. He was so mad that he jumped up and down.   _____

5. He had just obtained the car.   _____

I BODY SYSTEMS

Write **bronchial tubes, lungs,** or **trachea** in each blank.

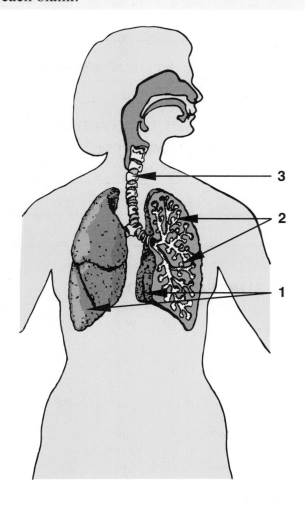

1. _____

2. _____

3. _____

J BODY SYSTEMS

Fill in each blank.

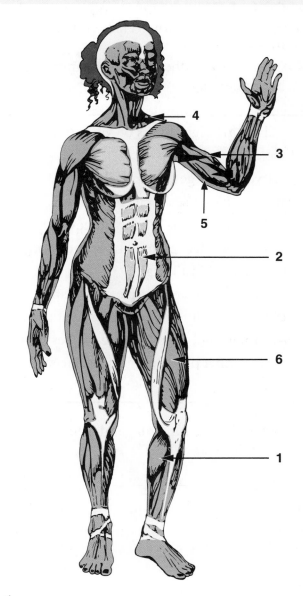

1. _____

2. _____

3. _____

4. _____

5. _____

6. _____

K INFERENCE

Read the story and answer the questions.
- Circle the **W** if the question is answered by words in the story. Then underline those words.
- Circle the **D** if the question is answered by a deduction.

> There are eight kinds of vitamin B. One kind is vitamin B-1.
>
> If you don't get vitamin B-1, you can get a bad disease called **beriberi** (BER-ry-BER-ry). When you have beriberi, you feel pain all over your body, and you can't walk right.
>
> Years ago lots of people got beriberi because they did not get enough vitamin B-1. Today, not many people get beriberi, but it is still a problem in some parts of the world.

1. What disease can you get if you don't get vitamin B-1?

   _____ **W** **D**

2. If Tom never gets vitamin B-1 and Wanda gets lots of vitamin B-1, which person may get beriberi?

   _____ **W** **D**

3. What happens to your body if you get beriberi?

   _____

   _____

   _____

4. How long ago did lots of people get beriberi?

   _____ **W** **D**

5. Why did people get beriberi?

   _____

   _____

   _____

L SUBJECT/PREDICATE

Circle the subject.

1. My left femur hurts.
2. My left femur and my right humerus hurt.
3. His little sister eats apples.
4. The cracked coffee cup was in the sink.
5. People stay inside when it rains.
6. Her heart was weak.
7. His heart, veins, and arteries were weak.
8. The heart pumps blood to all parts of the body.

M ANALOGIES

Write what each analogy tells.

> • where you find each part
> • what body system each part is in
> • what each part does

1. Gastrocnemius is to lower leg as bronchial tubes are to inside the lungs.

_____

_____

2. Gastrocnemius is to muscular system as bronchial tubes are to respiratory system.

_____

_____

N DEFINITIONS

Write a word that comes from **regulate** in each blank. Then write **verb, noun,** or **adjective** after each item.

1. That thermostat _____

   the heat in this room.

   _____

2. A _____

   department plans to raise your taxes.

   _____

3. Some _____ are hard to

   understand. _____

4. Those signal lights _____

   traffic. _____

5. The heart _____ the flow of

   blood to the arteries. _____

WORD LIST
bronchial tubes (n) the tubes inside the lungs
lung (n) a large organ that brings air into contact with the blood
produce (v) to make
production (n) something that is produced
productive (a) that something produces a lot of things
regulate (v) to control
regulation (n) a rule
respiratory system (n) the body system that brings oxygen to the blood
trachea (n) the tube that brings outside air to the lungs

ERRORS	G	W	B	T

A CONTRADICTIONS

Tell which fact each statement relates to. Make each contradiction true.

> **A.** Ted wanted to make just his quadriceps bigger.
> **B.** A poisonous snake bit one of Ted's veins.

1. The poison went into his heart. _____

2. He wants to work on a
three-headed muscle. _____

3. The muscle covers the back of
his femur. _____

4. The poison was in his
circulatory system. _____

B SENTENCE COMBINATIONS

Underline the common part. Circle the sentence that tells **why.** Combine the sentences with **because.**

1. Fred's house was robbed.
Fred wants protection.

_____

_____

_____

2. Larry wanted strong quadriceps.
Larry ran every day.

_____

_____

_____

3. The man rubbed his arm.
The man had a sore triceps.

_____

_____

_____

4. The veins can carry blood.
The veins are tubes.

_____

_____

_____

C SUBJECT/PREDICATE

Circle the subject.

1. Five ants were in a picnic basket.

2. Six men and a woman waited for the bus.

3. The dog was always tired in the afternoon.

4. They ran.

5. She ran to the store.

6. The bronchial tubes are inside the lungs.

7. Your femurs have to hold up the rest of your body.

8. The mouth takes in solid and liquid food.

D SENTENCE COMBINATIONS

Underline the common part. Then combine the sentences with **and.**

1. Ted started his car.
   Ted drove away.

   _____

   _____

2. Al has red pants.
   Marlene has red pants.

   _____

   _____

3. That man is crying.
   A baby is crying.

   _____

   _____

4. Her dog was drinking milk.
   His cat was drinking milk.

   _____

   _____

5. Linda likes to predict games.
   Tim likes to predict games.

   _____

   _____

6. A cat has white spots.
   Its kitten has white spots.

   _____

   _____

Lesson
35

E **INFERENCE**

Read the story and answer the questions.
- Circle the **W** if the question is answered by words in the story. Then underline those words.
- Circle the **D** if the question is answered by a deduction.

> You know that if you don't get any vitamin B–1, you can get a bad disease called beriberi. Rice has a lot of vitamin B–1. Not so long ago, people polished rice to make it look nicer. What these people did not know was that when they polished the rice, the rice lost all its vitamin B–1. People who ate only polished rice got beriberi. Today, people know that it's better to eat rice that isn't polished than to get beriberi. Rice that isn't polished is called brown rice.

1. What's the rule about vitamin B–1 and beriberi?

   _____

   _____

   _____

   _____ **W** **D**

2. What food has a lot of vitamin B–1?

   _____

3. Why did people polish rice?

   _____

   _____ **W** **D**

4. What happens to rice when you polish it?

   _____

5. What happened to people who ate only polished rice?

   _____ **W** **D**

6. What vitamin weren't those people getting?

   _____

7. Which is better, getting beriberi or eating rice that isn't polished?

   _____

   _____

F BODY SYSTEMS

Fill in each blank.

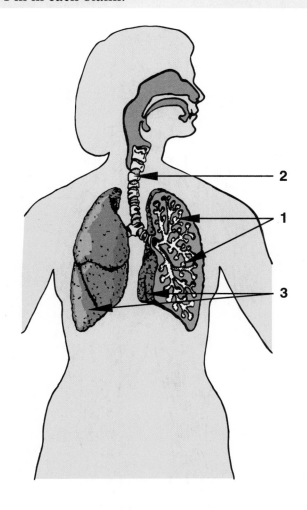

1. _____
2. _____
3. _____

G CONTRADICTIONS

Make each statement mean the same thing as the statement in the box.

> Running makes his quadriceps sore.

1. Running makes his arms hurt.
2. His lower leg muscles hurt when he runs.
3. When he runs, the muscles that cover his femur hurt.
4. Running makes muscles in his upper leg sore.

H FOLLOWING DIRECTIONS

Follow the directions.

> The quadriceps is a muscle that covers the _____ of the _____.

1. Fill in the blanks.
2. Cross out the part of **quadriceps** that means **four.**
3. Circle the part of **quadriceps** that means **heads.**
4. Make two lines over the articles.

I BODY SYSTEMS

Tell what body system each part is in.

1. Gastrocnemius is to the _____ system,

2. as humerus is to the _____ system,

3. as stomach is to the _____ system,

4. as trachea is to the _____ system,

5. as heart is to the _____ system.

J BODY SYSTEMS

Fill in each blank.

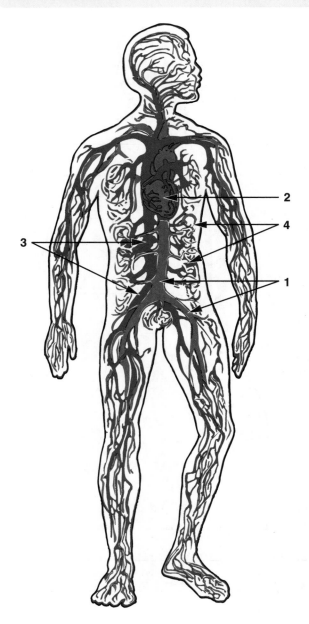

1. _____
2. _____
3. _____
4. _____

K SENTENCE COMBINATIONS

Underline the common part. Circle the word that combines the sentences correctly. Combine the sentences with that word.

1. Pete went hiking yesterday.
    Pete has a sore quadriceps.
    because   **who**   **which**

    _____

    _____

    _____

2. He predicted the rain.
    The rain came suddenly.
    and   **who**   **which**

    _____

    _____

3. The man is sick.
    His pet is sick.
    and   **who**   **which**

    _____

    _____

4. Gloria was drinking milk.
    Bob talked to Gloria.
    and   **who**   **which**

    _____

    _____

5. Fran has to stay healthy.
    Jim has to stay healthy.
    and   **who**   **which**

    _____

    _____

L EVIDENCE

Write **R** for each fact that is **relevant** to what happened. Write **I** for each fact that is **irrelevant** to what happened.

> Linda had big biceps.

1. She ran six miles a day.   _____

2. She did pull-ups.   _____

3. She did leg lifts.   _____

4. She had to bend her arms
    when she worked.   _____

M DEFINITIONS

Write a word that comes from **produce** or **criticize** in each blank. Then write **verb, noun,** or **adjective** after each item.

1. That tall woman is too

   _____ of other people.

   _____

2. His play was a costly _____.

   _____

3. Tom's father gives him a lot of

   helpful _____.

   _____

4. It takes lots of money to

   _____ a film.

   _____

5. Her factory is more _____

   than mine. _____

N DEDUCTIONS

Use the rule to answer the questions.

> The bigger the artery, the more blood it can carry.

1. Your leg artery is bigger than your arm artery.
   a. Which artery can carry more blood?

   _____

   _____

   b. How do you know?

   _____

   _____

2. The lung artery is one inch around. The heart artery is two inches around.
   a. Which artery can carry more blood?

   _____

   _____

   b. How do you know?

   _____

   _____

Glossary

A

abdominal muscle (n) the muscle that goes from the ribs to the pelvis

adjective (n) a word that comes before a noun and tells about the noun

arteries (n) the tubes that carry blood away from the heart

B

biceps (n) the muscle that covers the front of the humerus

brain (n) the organ that lets you think and feel

bronchial tubes (n) the tubes inside the lungs

C

capillaries (n) the very small tubes that connect the arteries and veins

circulatory system (n) the body system that moves blood around the body

construct (v) to build

construction (n) something that is constructed

constructive (a) that something is helpful

critical (a) that something criticizes

criticism (n) a statement that criticizes

criticize (v) to find fault with

D

digestive system (n) the body system that changes food into fuel

E

esophagus (n) the tube that goes from the mouth to the stomach

examine (v) to look at

F

femur (n) the upper leg bone

G

gastrocnemius (n) the muscle that covers the back of the lower leg

H

heart (n) the pump that moves the blood

humerus (n) the upper arm bone

I

irrelevant (a) that something does not help explain what happened

L

large intestine (n) the organ that stores food the body cannot use

liver (n) the organ that makes chemicals that break food down

lung (n) a large organ that brings air into contact with blood

M

mouth (n) the part that takes solid and liquid food into the body

muscular system (n) the body system of muscles

N

noun (n) a word that names a person, place, or thing

O

obtain (v) to get

P

pelvis (n) the hip bone

predict (v) to say that something will happen

predictable (a) that something is easy to predict

prediction (n) a statement that predicts

produce	(v) to make
production	(n) something that is produced
productive	(a) that something produces a lot of things
protect	(v) to guard
protection	(n) something that protects
protective	(a) that something protects

Q

quadriceps	(n) the muscle that covers the front of the femur

R

regulate	(v) to control
regulation	(n) a rule
regulatory	(a) that something regulates
relevant	(a) that something helps explain what happened
respiratory system	(n) the body system that brings oxygen to the blood
ribs	(n) the bones that cover the organs in the chest

S

select	(v) to choose
selection	(n) something that is selected
selective	(a) that something is careful about selecting things

skeletal system	(n) the body system of bones
skull	(n) the bone that covers the brain
small intestine	(n) the organ that gives food to the blood
spinal cord	(n) the body part that connects the brain to all parts of the body
spine	(n) the backbone
stomach	(n) the organ that mixes food with chemicals
subject	(n) the part of a sentence that names

T

trachea	(n) the tube that brings outside air to the lungs
trapezius	(n) the muscle that covers the back of the neck
triceps	(n) the muscle that covers the back of the humerus

V

veins	(n) the tubes that carry blood back to the heart
verb	(n) a word that tells the action that things do

A Complete the deductions.

1. Every dog has ribs. Bowser is a dog.

So, _____

2. Some trees are evergreens. A birch is a tree.

So, _____

_____

B Write the letter of the fact that explains why each thing happened.

A. On Monday, it was sunny.
B. On Tuesday, it was raining.

1. People went to the beach. _____

2. You could see your shadow. _____

3. The streets got wet. _____

C Write the class name for each group of objects.

1. Car, bike, truck _____

2. Hammer, screwdriver, pliers _____

D Answer the questions.

1. What's another word for **build?**

_____

2. What's another word for **look at?**

_____

3. What's another word for **guard?**

_____

E Answer the questions about the sentence.

The thirsty cat drank lots of water.

1. What's the part that names?

_____

2. What's the noun in the part that names?

_____

3. What's the verb in the part that tells more?

_____

F Read the sentence and answer the questions.

The painter broke one of her ribs when she fell off the ladder.

1. What did the painter break?

_____

2. In what body system was the part the painter broke?

_____

_____

3. What did the painter fall off of?

_____

G Complete each sentence with a word that comes from **select.**

1. Those shoppers are _____ new shirts at the store.

2. Tim needs to _____ a book to read.

H Follow the directions.

[ ]

1. Draw a big circle in the box.

2. Draw a vertical line from the top of the circle to the bottom of the circle.

3. Draw a horizontal line from the middle of the left side of the circle to the middle of the right side of the circle.

I Fill in each blank.

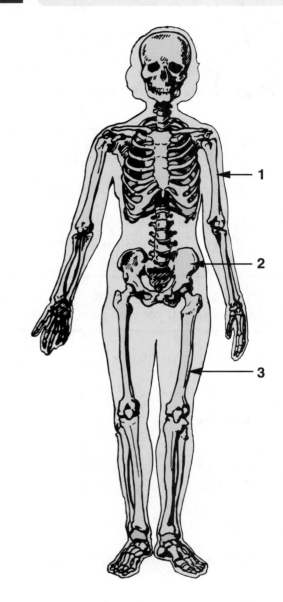

1. _____

2. _____

3. _____

A Use the rule to answer the questions.

| The bigger the ball, the easier it is to hit. |

1. A softball is bigger than a hardball. Which one is easier to hit?

_____

2. How do you know it is easier to hit?

_____

_____

B Complete the analogy.

| A hammer is to tools |

1. as a pig is to _____

_____

2. as a jet is to _____

3. as a shirt is to _____

_____

_____

C Answer the questions.

1. What's the adjective that means **that something is careful about selecting things?**

_____

2. What's the noun that means **something that is selected?** _____

3. What's the verb that means **build?**

_____

D Answer the questions.

1. What's the organ that makes chemicals that break food down?

_____

2. What's the organ that stores food the body cannot use?

_____

E Complete each sentence by writing a word that comes from **construct** or **select.** Then write **verb, noun,** or **adjective** after each item.

1. The carpenter used nails and a hammer to

_____ that shed.

_____

2. The _____ shopper stayed in the store for three hours.

_____

3. A skyscraper is a giant

_____ made of glass

and steel. _____

F Answer the questions about the sentence.

> The green dragon breathed red fire and black smoke.

1. What are the nouns in the sentence?

   _____

2. What are the adjectives?

   _____

3. What is the verb?

   _____

G Answer the questions about the sentence.

> The man sat at his desk.
> The man wrote a story.

1. What is the common part of those sentences?

   _____

2. Combine those sentences with **and.**

   _____

   _____

H Read the story and answer the questions.

> Britney was riding her bike home from school. Suddenly, she hit a big hole. She fell off her bike and broke her left humerus. She had to wear a cast for eight weeks. She also had to find another way to travel to and from school.

1. What bone did Britney break?

   _____

   _____

2. In what part of her body was that bone located?

   _____

   _____

3. Why couldn't Britney ride her bike to school for eight weeks?

   _____

   _____

I Fill in each blank.

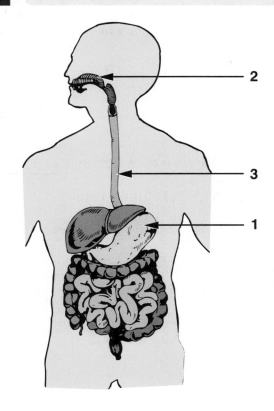

1. _____

2. _____

3. _____

A For each item, cross out the words that are in the rule and the conclusion. Then write the middle part.

1. Some boys have brown hair.

   _____

   So, maybe <u>Josh</u> has <u>brown hair</u>.

2. Every pine tree is an evergreen.

   _____

   So, a <u>pinyon</u> is an <u>evergreen</u>.

B Write **R** for each fact that is **relevant** to what happened. Write **I** for each fact that is **irrelevant** to what happened.

| The girl walked two miles to school. |

1. Her name was Sandy. _____

2. Her family's car was broken. _____

3. Her bicycle had a flat tire. _____

C Complete the analogies.

1. **Tell what system each body part is in.**

   Trapezius is to the _____ system

   as **femur** is to the _____ system.

2. **Tell where each body part is located.**

   Trapezius is to your _____

   as **femur** is to your _____.

D Make each statement mean the same thing as the statement in the box.

| The man had clogged arteries. |

1. The tubes that carried blood back to the man's heart were clogged.

2. Part of the man's digestive system was clogged.

E Answer the questions about the picture.

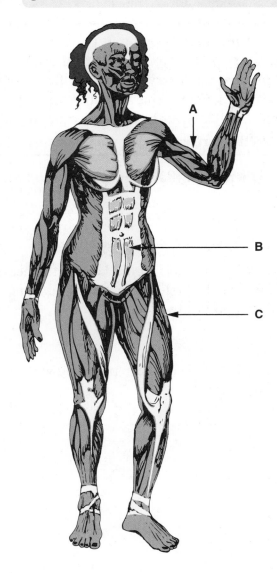

1. What is the name of muscle A?

_____

2. What is the name of muscle B?

_____

3. What is the name of muscle C?

_____

F Answer the questions about the picture.

1. Which bone will move: the top bone or the bottom bone?

_____

2. Which direction will the bone move: to the right or to the left?

_____

G Write a word that comes from **reside** or **criticize** in each blank. Then write **verb, noun,** or **adjective** after each item.

1. That lucky dog now _____

in a carpeted house. _____

2. The teacher made many _____

remarks on Fred's test. _____

H Answer the questions about the sentence.

> The tall painter brushed green paint on a canvas.

1. What are the nouns in that sentence?

_____

2. What are the articles?

_____

3. What is the verb?

_____

I For each pair of sentences, underline the common part. Then combine the sentences with **who** or **which.**

1. Debby lived in Miami.
   Miami is a city in Florida.

_____

_____

_____

2. She went to visit her uncle.
   Her uncle is very old.

_____

_____

J Read the passage and answer the questions.

> Your heart is a pump. It pumps blood to every part of your body. Your arteries are tubes that carry blood away from your heart, and your veins are tubes that carry blood back. Your heart keeps pumping all the time.

1. Where does your heart pump blood to?

_____

_____

2. Pretend you are a blood cell in the heart. What's the first kind of tube you enter after you leave the heart?

_____

3. Does your heart keep pumping when you are asleep?

_____

A   Complete the analogies.

1. Tell what noun comes from each verb.

Regulate is to _____

as **criticize** is to _____.

2. Tell what each verb means.

Regulate is to _____

as **criticize** is to _____.

B   Write **R** after each fact that is **relevant** to what happened. Write **I** after each fact that is **irrelevant** to what happened.

> The woman coughed for several minutes.

1. Her bronchial tubes weren't working properly. _____

2. Her arteries were filled with blood. _____

3. She had capillaries in her small intestine. _____

C   Answer the questions about the picture.

1. Which bone will move, the **top bone** or the **bottom bone**?

_____

2. Which direction will the bone move, to the **right** or to the **left?**

_____

D Answer the questions about the picture

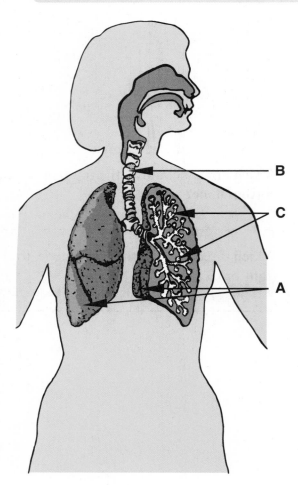

E Tell which fact each statement contradicts. Make each contradiction true.

> A. The triceps covers only the back of the humerus.
> B. Only your triceps straightens your arm.

1. The back of the upper leg bone is covered by the triceps. _____

2. The muscle on the back of the humerus straightens your neck. _____

3. A two-headed muscle straightens your arm. _____

F Write the conclusion of each deduction.

1. Some girls are named Mary. Fred has a sister.

So, _____

_____.

2. People cannot fly. A grebe is a bird.

So, _____.

1. What's the name of part A?

_____

2. What's the name of part B?

_____

3. What's the name of part C?

_____

G For each definition, write the word it defines.

1. A verb that means **control.**

   _____

2. An adjective that means **that something criticizes.**

   _____

3. A noun that means **a statement that predicts.**

   _____

4. A noun that means **the pump that moves the blood.**

   _____

5. An adjective that means **that something is helpful.**

   _____

H Follow the directions.

> The respiratory system brings oxygen to the blood.

1. Circle the subject.

2. Underline the last noun in the sentence.

3. Draw a line over the second article in the sentence.

4. Cross out the verb.

I For each pair of sentences, underline the common part and circle the sentence that tells **why.** Then combine the sentences with **because.**

1. The woman scraped her knee.
   The woman put on a bandage.

   _____

   _____

   _____

2. Alfred has a sore trapezius.
   Alfred twisted his neck.

   _____

   _____

   _____

J Use the rule to answer the questions.

> The heavier the box, the harder it is to lift.

Box A weighs 20 pounds, and Box B weighs 30 pounds.

1. Which box is harder to lift? _____

2. How do you know? _____

_____

K Complete each sentence by writing a word that comes from **regulate** or **produce.** Then tell if that word is a **verb, noun,** or **adjective.**

1. Driving _____ are rules

you have to follow. _____

2. That factory _____ hundreds

of cars last year. _____

3. It is hard to _____ the way

children behave. _____

L Read each analogy and question. Then circle the letter of the correct answer.

1. **Trachea** is to respiratory as **capillaries** are to circulatory. What does that analogy tell?
a. What bone each part covers.
b. What body system each part is in.
c. What verb comes from each noun.

2. **Produce** is to **make** as **regulate** is to **control.** What does that analogy tell?
a. What each verb means.
b. What verb comes from each noun.
c. What part of speech each word is.

M Write the middle part of each deduction.

1. Many body parts have capillaries.

_____

So, maybe the lungs have capillaries.

2. Cats do not have feathers.

_____

So, Felix does not have feathers.

N Complete the instructions.

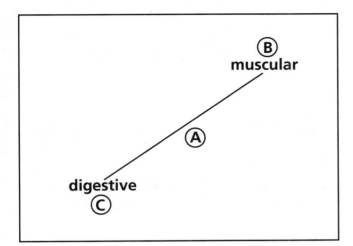

a. Draw a line that slants up to the

_____.

b. Write the word _____ above

the _____ end of the line.

c. Write the word _____ below

the _____ end of the line.

O For each pair of sentences, underline the common part and circle the word that combines the sentences correctly. Then combine the sentences with that word.

1. Main Street was lined with trees.
   The boy walked down Main Street.
   and   who   which

   _____

   _____

   _____

2. Veneta was very fond of her uncle.
   Her uncle was a firefighter.
   and   who   which

   _____

   _____

   _____

End-of-Program Test

> The tiny capillaries connect arteries and veins.

1. What are the nouns in that sentence?

_____

_____

2. What is the verb?

_____

3. What are the articles?

_____

4. What are the adjectives?

_____

> There are eight kinds of B vitamins. One kind is vitamin B-3.
>
> If you don't get vitamin B-3, you can get a disease called **pellagra** (puh-LAG-ruh). When you have pellagra, your skin gets rough, and your tongue swells up.
>
> You can get vitamin B-3 by eating fish, green vegetables, lean meat, milk, and eggs. Vitamin B-3 is also added to many breakfast cereals.

1. Vitamin B-3 is one kind of vitamin B. How many other kinds of vitamin B are there?

_____

2. What are two signs that somebody might have pellagra?

_____

_____

3. Which one of these vegetables has vitamin B-3: carrots, lettuce, or potatoes?

_____

4. How do you know that vegetable has vitamin B-3?

_____

_____

Answer Key for Fact Game 1

2. a. vehicles
   b. containers
   c. vehicles
   d. containers
   e. vehicles

3. a. The dog protected the yard.
   b. The man will obtain lumber.

4. a. obtain
   b. select

5. a. The doctor examined the bone.
   b. She will select a new dress.

6. Every car is a vehicle. A convertible is a car. So, a convertible is a vehicle.

7. a. A small red car
   b. car

8. a. skull
   b. ribs
   c. spine

9. Some bones are long. An ulna is a bone. So, maybe an ulna is long.

10. a. containers
    b. vehicles
    c. vehicles
    d. containers
    e. containers

11. skeletal system

12. a. protect
    b. examine

Answer Key for Fact Game 2

2. digestive system

3. A pencil is to writing as a book is to reading.

4. All birds have feathers. A dingo is not a bird. So, nothing.

5. a. containers
   b. animals
   c. tools

6. a. The dentist examined my teeth.
   b. Their dog protects the yard.

7. Most fruits grow on trees. Mangoes are fruits. So, maybe mangoes grow on trees.

8. a. adjective
   b. noun

9. A bird is to flying as a frog is to hopping (or leaping).

10. a. His, two, green
    b. The, young, a, new

11. a. We need to select a new car.
    b. Bill is obtaining a bottle of water.

12. a. stomach
    b. mouth
    c. esophagus

Answer Key for Fact Game 3

2. a. the rule
   b. the conclusion

3. a. predictable
   b. constructive
   c. selective

4. item b

5. a. muscular system
   b. skeletal system
   c. digestive system

6. a. reside
   b. prediction
   c. constructive

7. Ahmed and Narmeen reside in a big city.

8. a. adjective
   b. verb
   c. noun

9. a. predicted
   b. predictable
   c. predicting

10. a. bananas, peel
    b. ripe, a, yellow
    c. have

11. The driver slowed down and made a left turn.

12. a. biceps
    b. abdominal muscle
    c. quadriceps